THE

Old Trea...

D0880419

THE *Living* CHURCH

Old Treasures, New Discoveries

CHRISTOPHER M. BELLITTO, PhD

Liguori
LIGUORI, MISSOURI

Imprimi Potest:
Harry Grile, CSsR, Provincial
Denver Province, The Redemptorists

Published by Liguori Publications
Liguori, Missouri 63057

To order, call 800-325-9521, or visit liguori.org

Copyright © 2011 Christopher M. Bellitto

All rights reserved. No part of this publication may be reproduced, stored in a retrieval system, or transmitted in any form or by any means—electronic, mechanical, photocopy, recording, or any other—except for brief quotations in printed reviews, without the prior written permission of Liguori Publications.

Library of Congress Cataloging-in-Publication Data

Bellitto, Christopher M.
 The living Church : old treasures, new discoveries / Christopher M. Bellitto.—1st ed.
    p. cm.
  ISBN 978-0-7648-2039-7
  1. Catholic Church—History. I. Title.
  BX945.3.B44 2011
  282.09—dc22
                        2011011071

Scripture texts in this work are taken from the *New American Bible*, revised edition © 2010, 1991, 1986, 1970 Confraternity of Christian Doctrine, Inc., Washington, D.C. All Rights Reserved.

Some of this material first appeared as *Ten Ways the Church has Changed* by Christopher M. Bellitto (Boston: Pauline Books & Media, 2006).

Liguori Publications, a nonprofit corporation, is an apostolate of the Redemptorists. To learn more about the Redemptorists, visit Redemptorists.com.

Compliant with *The Roman Missal*, third edition.

Printed in the United States of America
15 14 13 12 11 / 5 4 3 2 1
First Edition

Contents

In fond and grateful memory of
Lawrence Boadt, CSP (1942–2010):
Teacher, scholar, editor, publisher,
but above all a kind man and a gentle priest

Preface

THIS BOOK ISN'T meant to be a complete history of the Church. Rather, it's intended to explore seven key aspects of the Church's life. Its goal is simple: to demonstrate briefly how the Church, over the course of two thousand years, has developed these seven aspects in the face of changing circumstances and diverse contexts. These are not the only seven aspects of the Church's life that are important, of course, but they are essential and allow us to see the process of development at work. They also permit the student of Church history to see the Church working at the top of her hierarchy, in the pews, and in the several layers of men and women in between. Church history, after all, not only trickles down but bubbles up, too.

We'll begin with three essentials: how she's organized as a structured institution, how her sacred writings came to be set into an authoritative canon (and who says so), and how beliefs were codified into doctrine. Then we'll pursue how the Church lives by looking at how the Mass developed, followed by the path to seven sacraments—a pair of chapters that are linked since Catholics celebrate sacraments in the context of liturgy. We'll consider how the Church has related with other faiths, which we should say up front is a troubling and difficult part of Church history. But it's also a chapter with some surprises, advances, and opportunities as we live in a world of truly global interaction at the start of the Church's third millennium. Finally, we'll explore how being a layperson has evolved over the centuries, sometimes dramatically and with profound implications for today and tomorrow.

Change is not new in Church history; it didn't start with Martin Luther in 1517 or Vatican II in the 1960s. It's important to remember that there was no catechism, code of canon law, complete Bible, or list of seven sacraments that came flying down from heaven after Jesus returned to his Father on ascension Thursday. Statements of what the Church teaches and how she will celebrate her faith and beliefs took time to come into being. While doctrine doesn't change, the way the Church explains doctrine and lives the faith does. To put it another way: divine law doesn't change, but human law changes frequently. The challenge is to know the difference and to make sure that change and development begin from real roots and grow organically, authentically, and within the appropriate authority system. Studying Church history helps us figure out what can and can't develop, what should and shouldn't change, whether developments happened too quickly or slowly, and whether change was explained well or not.

Change and development can be two very different things, of course, but they aren't unrelated. Often, a change looks like just that: something new. But as you study Church history, what we often find is that what's billed as change is in fact development—sometimes very slowly and over time—but in other cases, the Church has indeed switched gears. We can call this organic development, and we find that Church traditions, beliefs, and practices often evolve naturally, if sometimes fluidly, and at other times in fits and starts. Some very good recent studies have demonstrated, for example, how the Church first opposed freedom of conscience and usury, but then permitted these practices. On the other hand, the Church at one time permitted slavery in certain circumstances, but has now long been opposed to it and is a world leader in human rights discussions. Even something like the creation of a papal monarchy in the Middle Ages, which most historians call a papal revolution, had its seeds in ideas and practices from centuries before. And, of course, there is still a vibrant discussion about whether Vatican II's renewal (*aggiornamento*) represented a break with the past, continuity with prior traditions, or some creative combination. The Church's best scholars are still working on this recent history by using intriguing and nuanced phrases that really make you think: development or discontinuity in continuity, continuity in development, novelty in continuity, innovation within tradition, revolutionary evolution, and evolutionary revolution. You'll find examples of many of these combinations in this book.

A note about this book

THIS BOOK REWORKS a prior book of mine, *Ten Ways the Church has Changed* (Boston: Pauline Books & Media, 2006), but it covers some new material, is structured differently, and has been rewritten and edited in a number of ways. I edited and added to four chapters, combined four other chapters into two, added a new chapter on Scripture, reconceived other material into an epilogue, and left out two other chapters, though I drew on them here and there. I've also added discussion questions in the hope that this book might be used in parish religious education programs or reading circles.

I'm grateful to Father Mathew Kessler, CSsR, and Luis Medina of Liguori Publications and to the Liguori production and marketing teams for making this book happen. Finally, and as always, I thank Karen Bellitto, my wife and my best friend, for being her and for helping me be me.

CHAPTER 1

An Organized Church

HOW SHE OPERATES

In the beginning, local but linked

The subject of how the Church is organized and operates is related to the branch of theology known as ecclesiology: the nature, structure, and function of the Church. Not surprisingly, we soon come to the question of who is in charge of the Church and just as quickly to conflicting answers. To begin, when we think about the early Church, today's model has to be the furthest thing from our minds. There was no centralized papacy in the first centuries after Jesus, but rather a series of local Churches, each of which gradually came to be led by one bishop. Perhaps the best image is that of a chain of islands—an archipelago of Christian communities spread across the Mediterranean shores—each of which was generally independent, but often in contact with others. The communities sent letters of encouragement and questions to each other. When Christians traveled, they surely sought out other Christians in the towns they visited, for safety if nothing else, because Christianity was still an underground and illegal religion before the early fourth century.

In this context, several developments occurred slowly. The first concerned the organization of the new Christians. Since the first Christians were Jews, it was natural to adapt the synagogue's model of elders, readers, and those who cared for the material needs of the congregation. For a time, the word synagogue (gathering) was used alongside *ekklesia* (Church or assembly). As Christianity moved away from Judaism, particular Christian offices emerged: bishops, priests, and deacons—who were sometimes grouped together as elders—and then lectors, catechists, and others. Elders were sometimes called by the Latin word *saniores* (the older or wiser ones) and appear to have originally been lay leaders who oversaw the community. After the third century, as ordination developed more formally, this category of elders dropped away.

The second development was monepiscopacy: each community gathered under the leadership and direction of one man, the local bishop, who personified the community. During the sporadic persecutions by the Roman Empire's authorities, it was often the bishop who was killed in the hope that the community would be decapitated—but Christianity continued to grow, to the Romans' disappointment and amazement. The bishop (*episkopos*, borrowing the word for a supervisor or inspector) traced his heritage and authority to the original apostles. He played several roles: administrative leader, chief preacher, judge, and central liturgical celebrant. We hear of the bishop's importance in a letter written by Ignatius, the bishop of Antioch, who was martyred in Rome around 110–117. Writing to the Christian community in Smyrna, he advised: "Apart from the bishop let no one do anything pertaining to the Church," adding a moment later, "Let the people be present wherever the bishop appears, just as the Catholic Church is wherever Jesus Christ is." In each community, one liturgy was celebrated each Sunday, further linking the bishop with the Eucharist as the unifying center of the Church's body.

Did this mean bishops were all on an equal footing and did not come under other bishops? The answer depended on who you asked. For Cyprian, the bishop of Carthage in north Africa who died as a martyr in 258, the episcopacy "is one; the individual members have each a part, and the parts make up the whole." Cyprian considered the bishop of Rome the source of the episcopacy because of Peter's designation by Christ as the origin of unity. But for Cyprian, "certainly the other apostles were what Peter was, endowed with an equal fellowship both of honor and power; but the beginning is made from unity, that the Church of Christ may be shown to be one." Cyprian was not always so diplomatic in striking this delicate balance. In 256, he led a council in north Africa that challenged Stephen I, the bishop of Rome (254–257). Cyprian stressed that Peter had not claimed supremacy over Paul nor required obedience. He complained that the bishop of Rome had set himself up as a kind of autocratic and intimidating bishop of bishops. This council asserted that the

Roman bishop could confirm their decisions on appeal, but Rome could not reverse them. Intervention was certainly not welcome, and we see this in the language of the bishops' letters. Many bishops addressed each other—including the bishops of Rome—as brother, but Damasus I (366–384) of Rome called bishops his sons.

A third development occurred in Rome that both complemented and challenged monepiscopacy in the Christian archipelago. There was a sense that Peter's mandate from Christ and his presence in the empire's capital gave that city a special role. It was not uncommon for Christian bishops outside Rome to disagree with the bishop of Rome in this period, as Cyprian did, but the bishop of Rome was steadily developing toward a more central and dominating role. Supporters of Roman authority stated that a bishop's power of the keys passed through Rome, just as Peter passed the authority that Christ had given to him along to the other apostles. This argument said that, while local bishops have pastoral responsibility for their part of the Church, it is the bishop of Rome who has the ultimate and full pastoral responsibility for the entire Church.

Callistus I (217–222) was the first bishop of Rome to invoke Petrine authority explicitly, for example, and Stephen I used the phrase *cathedra Petri* (seat or chair of Peter) to describe his own place in Rome. Julius I (337–352) was angry when bishops who had gathered at Antioch in 341 did not inform him of their deliberations and actions. Julius wrote to them: "Do you not realize that it has been the custom for word to be sent to us first, that in this way just decisions may be arrived at from this place [Rome]?" Two years later, in 343, a local council at Sardica recognized Julius' authority and right of appeal. By the time of Innocent I (401–417), the bishop of Rome was declaring that nothing done by the clergy, no matter how far away they were from the imperial capital, could be considered settled definitively until the pope gave his approval.

A fourth development linked these others. As the Church grew larger and more extensive geographically, a system of organization modeled on that of the Roman Empire's dioceses (administrative regions) naturally had to develop. Gradually, an urban bishop was in charge of a local city as well as its surrounding rural district. Bishops of larger cities oversaw them; the most famous of these are the five patriarchates of Rome, Alexandria, Antioch, Jerusalem, and Constantinople. Four hundred years after Jesus' resurrection, then, Christianity had clearly come far from a small group of unorganized followers on the edge of the Roman Empire.

Medieval centralization

With the disintegration of the Roman Empire in the fifth century, the cities of Europe declined and the population moved into the countryside. Christianity's leaders, the bishops, took over civil leadership positions left by the Roman city officials while parishes also grew in rural areas. It was a time of growth and expansion for Christianity, but because of the empire's fall, communication slowed down and coordination among dioceses was not always efficient or extensive. In a sense, the archipelago had expanded, but also grew further apart. The advantage was that the old Roman administrative system was already in place. Into its power vacuum walked the Church and in particular her bishops, who adopted Roman law systems for their own use, the Roman *lingua franca* of Latin as the official language of the Church, and the Romans' organizational structure to administer a faith that was becoming the dominant belief system throughout Europe.

As these organizational developments occurred on the local level, the Church took steps to organize herself on a larger scale. Metropolitan bishops in charge of other bishops now came to be called archbishops. The bishops below them were suffragan bishops who came under their archbishop's authority, supervision, and jurisdiction. This system ensured that conflicts, questions, and appeals could be pursued in an orderly and fair manner up the hierarchical chain of authority. Once more, the Roman Empire's structure was filled in by Christianity. Just as Roman dioceses became Christian dioceses (first as neighborhoods and then as larger regions), the boundaries of the Roman provinces were roughly followed as the archbishops' provinces or spheres of authority. Provinces, in turn, were grouped into even larger regions. At the highest layers, even as popes were centralizing their authority, general councils were arguing—in the most extreme case—that a council and not a pope was the ultimate authority in the Church. What was at stake was the very organizing and unifying principle of the Church's structural life.

The papacy in the Middle Ages took a series of steps to consolidate its authority and power not only versus secular governments but also within the Church herself. Medieval popes wanted to be the ultimate executive, legislative, and judicial authorities within the body of the Church. One of the most important operational developments in this period was the college of cardinals, which popes used to spread the power of the papacy. Although cardinals had existed in some form for more than five hundred years, the medieval popes made the college more of an institution with certain rights and privileges—something like the ancient Roman Senate, a medieval royal curia, or today's presidential cabinet. Only the pope could name cardinals, and he increasingly appointed them from a broader geographic area throughout Europe. In the twelfth century alone, three hundred new cardinals were named, although there were usually only a few dozen at any one time. They became his inner circle in Rome and his voice as legates across Europe. As the papacy developed financial, legal, liturgical, and secretarial departments, the popes put cardinals in charge as their most trusted advisers, which made the college and curia training grounds for future popes.

The cardinals' most important role was to elect the pope. In 1059, Pope Nicholas II gave the cardinals the lead role in papal elections, although the major Roman families and even the sitting pope could make their preferences known and exercise some influence, as they'd done for several centuries. A general council, Lateran III in 1179, said that elections no longer had to be unanimous to be valid: a two-thirds majority would suffice for a candidate's election. Another council, Lyons II in 1274, gave the Church the conclave, which locked the cardinals away until they chose a pope. Not only was this measure intended as an attempt to cut off outside interference; it was also meant to speed the election along, as the Church had recently gone through nearly three years without a pope because the cardinals could not settle on one man.

Meanwhile, proponents of general councils were promoting the idea that the pope is a kind of delegated authority figure or chief executive officer, with the people of God as the ultimate authority in the Church. This, in turn, was based on an ecclesiology that said the Church was the mystical body of Christ (to use Paul's image in Corinthians). Practically speaking—to put it in less theological and more modern political terms—the people of God did not abdicate their sovereignty to the pope but looked to him and their bishops to exercise leadership in their name without ever becoming unaccountable. On another level, since everyone could not participate in Church matters, some type of representative institution must voice the people's concerns in an orderly and efficient manner. This is what led to the upsurge in conciliarism, whose several versions assigned varying exercises of authority to the pope. The fundamental questions ran on a handful of interlocking levels: how to balance the bishop of Rome as the successor to Peter with the bishops of other places as successors to the apostles with the power of the college of cardinals with the history of councils that helped run the Church since her first centuries. The goal was somehow to balance the singular authority of the pope with the corporate nature of the Church as the mystical body of Christ with many members gathered around and unified by the Eucharist.

There is a clear crossover here with some emerging secular developments, such as Magna Carta (1215), which talked about trials by jury, due process, and a king bound by the consent of those he governed. Parliaments in England were developing as challenges to royal authority, and the same was true of representative institutions throughout Europe, with different degrees of success. Especially in Italy, city-states modeled on the ancient Greek *polis* as well as communes experimented with representative governments. However, there is a long Church history of representation and participation, as well. Monks and nuns had, for centuries, made decisions together in their monasteries and convents, even up to the point of electing their own abbots and abbesses. Religious orders like the Dominicans had done the same since the early thirteenth century. In some cities, priests elected their own bishops, as cardinals elected the popes.

Conciliar activity and authority was not a medieval innovation or heresy. Throughout the first thousand years of the Church, councils on the local, regional, and universal levels had met to consider the great theological and disciplinary questions of the day. The earliest—Nicaea in 325—was called not by a pope but by the emperor Constantine, yet its creed set the standard for what Christians say they believe about Jesus. Other general councils had little or no papal participation, although popes gradually played a larger role in the eight ecumenical councils that met in the first millennium. What changed in the Middle Ages was that popes tried to control the general councils: indeed, four Lateran councils met in the pope's own palace in Rome in 1123, 1139, 1179, and 1215. These were very papal events, but when the papacy began to lose its moral authority and become bogged down in pomp and politics, general councils stepped in to claim increased authority. The bottom fell out during the Great Western Schism (1378–1417) when two and then three papacies (and subsequently two and then three colleges of cardinals) competed for power.

Into this debate stepped the General Council of Constance (1414–1418), which continued to meet even after the pope who called it ran away in the middle of the night when it was clear he was going to be deposed and not reelected by the general council's representatives. In April 1415, Constance declared that the highest authority in the Church is a general council:

"This holy council of Constance…declares, first that it is lawfully assembled in the Holy Spirit, that it constitutes a general council, representing the Catholic Church, and that therefore it has its authority immediately from Christ; and that all men, of every rank and condition, including the pope himself, [are] bound to obey it in matters concerning the faith, the abolition of the schism, and the reformation of the church of God in its head and its members."

After deposing two of the three popes and forcing the third to resign, Constance oversaw the selection of a unifying pope, Martin V (1417–1431), who was elected by a one-time-only extension of voting beyond the usual colleges of cardinals to include conciliar representatives. Before adjourning, Constance tried to make general councils a regular and not extraordinary feature of the Church's life. A decree named *Frequens* stated that a general council must meet frequently: once every ten years. For the next three decades, popes fought with general councils and these assertions. A series of strong popes eventually fought back the conciliar challenge. Pope Pius II (ironically, a former conciliarist) in 1460 slammed conciliarists as "imbued with the spirit of rebellion" and condemned conciliarism as "this pestilent poison" and as "erroneous and destestable."

By the end of the Middle Ages, then, the papacy was once more reasserting its ultimate authority, although it was yet again damaging itself with political patronage and secular matters. Conciliarism struggled to reassert itself, but by the time the next general council met, at Trent (1545–1563), it was clearly a council of bishops under the pope's leadership, whose decisions had to be approved and promulgated by the pope, otherwise they would have had no authority whatsoever. These bishops threw their efforts into revitalizing the Church at its basic level—in parishes—and that is where they made their stand in helping the Church recover from the conciliar and Protestant challenges.

Any discussion of how the Church during the Reformations considered the question of ecclesiology and of how the Church should be organized and governed must take into account the competing Protestant ecclesiologies. Protestants sought to return the Church to its earliest models of decentralization, to greater participation by the laity, and (for those Protestant churches with bishops) to a role for the bishop that was fairly independent and certainly not under the authority of a pope. Catholics responded to the Protestant challenges by reasserting very strongly the very necessity and legitimacy of the episcopacy and especially the papacy. After the Council of Trent, a great deal of effort was spent on centralization in Rome. During these centuries, the Church was organized and governed under the leadership of Rome. The year after Trent adjourned in 1563, Rome issued a new index of forbidden books as well as a profession of faith that embodied the careful doctrinal language Trent had worked out to restate the faith in light of the Protestant challenges. A few years later, an official catechism was published to teach this faith.

To oversee this continuing centralization, popes in this period were selected for their administrative skills: most had canon law backgrounds, few had advanced training in theology. They emphasized their roles as absolute monarchs of the papal states, that is, as temporal rulers. When they turned their attention to spiritual matters, they took a more administrative and less pastoral approach, too. They were not, however, the scandalous Renaissance popes of the prior generation, and indeed they were largely successful in their attempts at reorganizing the Church. They demonstrate the fact that the papacy had to compete with other monarchies and bureaucracies of the age. As the Jesuit Robert Bellarmine put it early in the seventeenth century, the Church is a community just like the kingdom of France or the republic of Venice.

But we should quickly add that the Church's organization did not operate exclusively at the top during these centuries. Trent empowered bishops to implement its reform decrees and bring the Church back to life. The council had mandated that bishops live in their dioceses, since absenteeism had long been a problem and a legitimate complaint by both Catholic and Protestant reformers. Bishops had to meet in provincial councils under their archbishops once every three years; each individual diocese's clergy had to meet under its bishop in an annual synod. These meetings were uneven: there were a few in Germany, though a fair number met regularly in Spain and Italy.

The challenge was balancing local independence and culture with Roman centralization. At the local level, bishops were now more concerned with asserting orthodoxy and uniformity with respect to training priests, examining them before ordination, supervising them by visiting their parishes, and gathering their insights and concerns by meeting with them periodically. Their goal was to make the parish the center of life and oversight: they wanted to encourage spiritual liveliness but make sure it kept in line with orthodoxy. Parishes began to keep better records, particularly for baptisms and marriages. So, even though the emphasis was undoubtedly on how the Church was organized from the top down, this does not mean the Church was not operating well from the bottom up.

Monarchy and democracy

Church developments in the modern period starting about the seventeenth century were heavily influenced by increased secular political participation that led to revolutions against monarchies and more democratic governmental structures. There was also the Enlightenment's challenge to faith as a result of its increasing emphasis on reason and logic that sometimes pushed religion into the realms of ignorance and superstition. This challenge was compounded by the secularism and materialism that accompanied the Industrial Revolution, first in England, then across Europe, and ultimately in the new United States, starting in New England and spreading across the fast-growing country. To defend herself against these challenges, the Church increasingly stressed her hierarchy, specifically at the upper-most level of the papacy, and emphasized her authority to patrol doctrine and discipline. This approach frustrated some Catholics who were participating in their secular governments but could not do so in a similar way in their Church. What dominated discussions of how the Church should be organized and operate was the question of whether the Church was fundamentally different from other governments or institutions. It dealt with matters not only of this world but also beyond it, so should it be in dialogue with earthly political and social changes?

We have just heard Robert Bellarmine, the Jesuit theologian who was later named a cardinal, describe the Church as an institution as powerful and rooted in the world as France or Venice. His conception remained influential in the early modern period, as the Church continued to recover from the Reformations and then found herself under assault as just another monarchy, like the Bourbons overthrown during the French Revolution in 1789 or England's George III, who was deposed as head of the colonies during the American Revolution a decade earlier. But, for Bellarmine and others, the Church wasn't just another government. A phrase used frequently during this period was "perfect society": the Church was a perfect society, which did not mean it held no sinners among its millions of members around the world, but rather that it was a self-sustaining organization with its own hierarchy, system of government, rules of order, levels of administration, and allegiance of its members. Clearly, this notion of a perfect society, at least in this version of its description, was an institutional conception. The notion of the Church as a society set apart from others was resisted in the seventeenth and eighteenth centuries by European monarchs who tried to make the Church a department of their individual countries, and especially in France and Austria, where rulers wanted to make Catholicism a state Church. They wanted to name bishops, organize dioceses, assign priests, and oversee Churches and parochial schools.

In a similar way, there were some American Catholics who wanted not the Roman Catholic Church in America, but an American Church more closely adapted to American governmental structures. These ideas flourished not long after Americans had won their independence from Great Britain. The Bill of Rights in the new United States Constitution gave American Catholics, who existed in small numbers at the end of the eighteenth century, the freedom they had not enjoyed when the colonies were British and part of the Church of England. Lay Catholics exercised their newfound freedoms by practicing a Catholicism informed by the same fierce independence that had fueled the break from Great Britain. American Catholics, after all, were democratic Americans who had just overthrown a king's authority. They wanted to act as the people of the Church as they were now the people of the new United States.

This desire for self-determination played out in a movement called trusteeism. The issues were governance and authority. Who owned a parish? Who could buy and sell its property? Who could make decisions about a parish, its pastor, or its programs? What was the parish's relationship with its pastor and bishop? Lay Catholics making up a parish's board of trustees asserted they owned and controlled churches, schools, and even the priests assigned to them. They held that it was up to them to pay the bills, order and oversee new building projects or programs, and hire and fire employees from the parish secretary to its priests and pastor—some said bishop, too. They were happy to leave the sacraments to the priests, but that should be the end of the clergy's mandate.

Pastors and bishops disagreed. The resulting battles turned ugly as clergy and laity fought by using adversarial us-versus-them language of clericalism, anti-clericalism, and the hierarchy of vocations. Legal cases followed. Parishes and dioceses were split apart in cities with sizable and wealthy Catholic populations: New York City, Buffalo, Boston, Philadelphia, Baltimore, Norfolk, Charleston, and New Orleans. American bishops fought back in 1829 with a firm statement that they were in charge of parishes, had financial control of their dioceses and its properties, and held the exclusive right to hire and fire priests. Like bishops in other countries, American bishops saw this attempt to apply democracy or republicanism to the Church as a Protestant or congregationalist model that was not in keeping with Roman Catholic teaching and tradition. It was an uprising that the bishops felt they had to put down, which they successfully did in the 1830s–1850s, using Church and civil law to help them regain financial control of their parishes and dioceses.

So the Church's centralization was not without its resisters, inside and out. In response, the hierarchy tended to add yet another brick into the defensive posture and siege mentality that characterized the institutional Church's approach to the world during this period. Officials at the Church's highest levels spent their time making sure the Church's administrative structures were in order while defending Catholicism's monarch, the pope, against those inside the Church who wanted the Church to adapt to the democratic developments taking place outside the Church. So the Church became even more closed at its structural top, even as down below the Church was diversifying around the world.

Nevertheless, by the 1840s nearly every discussion of the Church's organization and government took place in institutional and administrative terms. The discussion was always about authority, but it was rarely even a discussion; it was more a statement of fact. A theologian named Giovanni Perrone, for example, stressed that the Church really meant the pope and his bishops gathered together as the Church's teachers. Her teaching authority, the magisterium, did not leave room for participation for speculative theologians or laypeople. It was the job of the pope and bishops to teach. It was the job of the people, the laity below the highest clergy, to learn. While laypeople received the Church's teaching, they were not in any way to question that teaching or participate in its formulation, acceptance or rejection, or subsequent reformulation.

Church organization and government certainly did not assign a central role to the laity. The idea that if the people did not receive a teaching it was not therefore a valid teaching was simply not tolerated even as a theoretical possibility. As a result, the notion of the people of God as the mystical body of Christ who participate in the formulation of doctrine by acting as a living check or proof of a doctrine's validity largely vanished. This idea, called the *sensus fidelium,* would have to wait until the end of the nineteenth century, and especially to the coming of Vatican II in the middle of the twentieth, to once again enjoy some acceptance, as it had done in the early and medieval centuries of the Church's development.

Indeed, major changes were at hand and the impetus to develop was coming from the Church's fingers and toes. European missionaries were gradually turning their parishes and dioceses over to indigenous catechists and ministers. Popes Benedict XV, Pius XI and Pius XII in the beginning and middle of the twentieth century were particularly supportive of missions. They wanted to see priests of the same ethnicities, cultures, and races as the parishioners they served. Ordinations to the priesthood of indigenous men rose sharply after 1915, and ordinations to the episcopacy naturally followed: six Chinese priests were ordained bishops by Pope Pius XI himself in Rome in 1926, then a Japanese bishop followed the next year, with a Korean bishop in 1937, and then the first modern African bishop in 1939. (There had been north African bishops during the early centuries, but once Islam took hold of north Africa in the seventh century, Christianity largely disappeared. While north Africa remains mostly Muslim today, large sections of sub-Saharan Africa are Christian and specifically Catholic.) Bishops from India and Indonesia soon followed.

The next important step in modern ecclesiology and discussions of Church organization and governance came in 1943 with Pope Pius XII's encyclical *Mystici corporis*. In this statement, Pius XII stressed the centrality of the pope as the representative of Christ, the Church's ultimate head, and the pope as successor to the chief apostle Peter, who is Christ's vicar on earth. The pope called the bishops "the more illustrious members of the Universal Church," but noted that they are subordinate to papal authority (no. 42). In the same encyclical, Pius XII also used more expansive theological language to talk about the Church as the mystical body of Christ, therefore resurrecting an idea from early and medieval ecclesiology. A hierarchy is at work, but it is not a question of a hierarchy or the mystical body, but instead a hierarchy and the mystical body—two ideas that do not compete and do not cancel each other out.

The road was now open to Vatican II and especially to the document *Lumen gentium*, which gathered all of these ideas together and tried to strike that delicate balance that had existed in varying degrees up until the late twentieth century. *Lumen gentium* spent time discussing the Church as the people of God and the mystical body of Christ, while also acknowledging the bishops' leadership and their role as the apostles' successors. *Lumen gentium* also acknowledged the primacy of the pope as both a member of the college of bishops and the college of bishops' head. Here we have a conception of the Church that is multi-layered and tries hard to balance centuries of various images, offices, notions, and experiences of how the Church should operate.

But we must acknowledge that questions remain. Some theologians support the papal centralization of John Paul II and Benedict XVI while others—bishops and cardinals among them—are concerned that they stressed the papacy too much at the expense of the local bishop, regional groups of bishops, and national episcopal conferences. Specifically, we hear complaints that synods of bishops have become nothing more than rubber stamps of decisions that the pope has already made. They would like a more participatory assembly or at least a larger role played by bishops and theologians. Still others are concerned that the very idea of collegiality—of the bishops as equal members of the worldwide brotherhood of bishops united especially as the Church's teachers—has been lost entirely. Another issue is subsidiarity: some bishops would like local decisions to be made locally, or at least in the context of a national episcopal conference, with no recourse to Roman approval. Once more, the question is: what is the relationship between the local Church and the pope in Rome? Ironically, then, the Church today finds herself asking many of the same questions she asked in her first centuries, but now she has many more years of experience, mistakes, achievements, and wisdom from which to draw as she moves forward.

Discussion questions

- Do you think the move from a decentralized to a centralized Church was inevitable? Wise? Reversible? Helpful and/or harmful?

- How do you think the Church is operating today on the local, national, and global levels? What is successful? What needs improvement—and how might that happen?

- What does the sacrament of baptism have to do with participation in Church matters generally? Specifically, what is the value in having the laity involved in decision-making when it comes to parish matters?

- Can you name a time when you felt the Church's structure and organization really did a good job in living out its mission of service?

- Can you name a time when you felt the Church's structure and organization failed in living out its mission of service? What went wrong and how could structures be corrected?

CHAPTER 2

Scripture

THE STARTING POINT

SOME OF THE FIRST MOMENTS of learning the Faith come from Bible stories. Long before children can read these stories by themselves, they hear them told or read to them by others, starting with their parents. But even to adults, Bible stories are not always clear—they can seem confusing, tricky, even disturbing—so someone has to explain the point of the story. And there, replicated every hour of every day around the globe, is how the Church shares her faith: not only by reading the Scriptures, but by applying them to daily life, explaining them to others, and figuring out how to put into today's language the Church's doctrines, structures, and practices that come from the word of God. So Scripture is indeed the starting point, but for Catholics, a process of explanation and teaching called Tradition follows almost immediately. As we track the history of scriptural development and interpretation, then, we will often find biblical words and the Church's teachings walking side by side.

Building the Bible

We have to remember that the collection of writing that we call the Bible, comprised of the Old Testament (sometimes referred to as Hebrew Scripture) and New Testament (Christian Scripture), was not settled immediately. The word "bible" comes from the Greek word *biblia* and indicates a library or a collection of books, which makes sense since, though we often call the Bible a holy book or the Good Book, it's actually an anthology of writings of many different literary genres: historical narratives, some biography, prose and poetry, letter and Gospel, prophecy and lamentation. There were many books available in the ancient world telling the story of the Hebrew people and of Jesus, and some of these were recognized as more authoritative than others over time, which created a canon.

The word "canon" comes from a Hebrew word sometimes translated as balance beam, cane, or measuring reed. It became a Greek word meaning a ruler—the standard by which other things are measured—and is related to the act of the Catholic Church canonizing a person, that is, making an authoritative statement that he or she is a saint. We also talk about Church law as canon law and the main part of the eucharistic prayer as the Mass's canon. So before we talk about how Jewish and Christian Scripture can be read and understood, we have to talk about its very existence as a group of writings that came to be accepted as the norm.

We are pretty sure that every word of the Bible began in the oral tradition, maybe as early as the thirteenth century BC. At some point, perhaps starting as soon as 1000 BC or so when David and Solomon built up a capital for their monarchy in Jerusalem, these stories and laws were written on scrolls. A collection referred to as the Law or Torah was taken as the norm by 400 BC, though it may have been written in bits and pieces starting around the seventh or sixth century BC. Books grouped as the Prophets were added about 200 BC. Then, other oral traditions and written scrolls that were in use were, in a sense, canonized by about 100 AD, including Psalms, Proverbs, Job, and the Song of Songs, known together as the Writings.

All of these books were translated into a Greek version called the *Septuagint*, which is the Latin word for the number seventy. According to legend, seventy (or seventy-two, in other versions) Jewish elders working separately in Alexandria identically translated the first five books of Hebrew Scripture called the Law or Pentateuch (Genesis, Exodus, Leviticus, Numbers, Deuteronomy). During the second century AD, the word *Septuagint* came to refer to all Jewish Scriptures, some of which had begun in Greek and not Hebrew. Still, there was no definitive grouping: the collection used in Palestine counted a short canon of thirty-nine books, which over time became the mainstream grouping among most Jews, while a long canon generally accepted in Alexandria included up to fifty-one books. This standardization of Hebrew texts was likely occurring because the new faith of Christianity was not only drawing on Jewish written tradition, typically the Greek *Septuagint* because most early Christians knew Greek, but also adding its own material in what came to be called the New Testament.

All of the New Testament writings were written in a much shorter period of time than the Old Testament. The New Testament was composed within a fifty-year period, starting within two decades of Jesus' passion. This period was the second half of the first century. In contrast, the composition of the Old Testament spanned as long as a millennium from about 1000 BC to shortly before Jesus' life. At first, there was no one group of Christian writings that everyone took as definitive, but rather there was a variety of circulating materials called *graphai* (writings). Paul refers to them and presumes that his listeners were familiar with these writings. His own writings formed part of the *graphai* that were gaining acceptance and his letters are, in fact, the very first parts of the accepted New Testament to have been written down, probably in the 50s AD. The Gospels almost certainly began in an oral tradition that, over time, were committed to writing about 70–100 AD, in the order of Mark, Matthew, Luke, and John. This may have happened because the very first Christians thought the world was soon going to end with Jesus' return, but when this didn't happen, they had to hand the Faith down, and written stories helped that process. So letters composed quickly and focused on issues of the day gave way to Gospels that told a longer story.

During the second and third centuries AD, two types of lists of Christian books emerged. The first list named books considered part of the emerging Christian collection. They were enjoying consensus as pieces of a canon of writings that contained the truth about Jesus and his teachings, especially his moral directives. A document called the Second Letter of Clement from Rome in the first half of the second century, for example, calls Matthew's Gospel part of the *graphai.* Not long before, a bishop of Antioch named Ignatius had referred to key passages from books clearly in common circulation: Matthew and John's Gospels along with letters attributed to Paul, including 1 Corinthians, Ephesians, Galatians, and Colossians. A second list identified false books containing untruths. These lists did not include Hebrew Scriptures, however, which were considered as a separate collection. By about 200, Christians were referring to the Old and New Testaments to distinguish these two collections.

How did Church authorities establish canonicity? It was, of course, necessary to do so because the Church was still illegal in the Roman Empire and there was no centralized authority to patrol orthodoxy—and, indeed, universal creeds did not exist yet. Some believers were taking parts of Jesus' message and rejecting others. Competing canons were in circulation, such as the one kept by Marcion, a second-century dissident who rejected any relationship between Jewish tradition and Christian writings because he saw the stereotypical angry God of the Old Testament as incompatible with the loving Son of the New Testament. Marcion accepted only Luke's Gospel from those being used, but he omitted the nativity narrative because he rejected Jesus' humanity. He also edited Paul to emphasize those strong passages that seemed to oppose ties with Judaism, and he removed references to the incarnation and passion because they treated the humanity that Marcion did not believe in.

About the same time, in a more positive fashion, an apologist named Tatian tried to harmonize the accounts of the four Gospels that were winning general acceptance and that were used most frequently. He tried to reconcile their discrepancies in a study called the *Diatessaron.* Origen, in the middle of the third century, drew up in his *Hexapla* parallel columns of text with Hebrew and various

Greek versions of scriptural passages in an effort to reconcile their dichotomies, too. The very fact that Tatian and Origen did this bears testimony to the fact that there was not yet an established New Testament canon nor an organized, unifying authority to oversee, accept, correct, or reject such an effort definitively.

As different people began to hold and teach different explanations of doctrine supported by evidence they selected from sacred writings—what we call proof texts—it became clear that there needed to be one standard set of Scripture. If the Church was to be catholic (universal), then everyone had to agree on standard writings and an accepted version and translation of them. By the middle of the 200s, we can say that there appeared to be some agreement on a canon of Christian writings accepted in most churches, and that this canon was fairly close to what became the standard New Testament.

Precisely what made one text canonical to be included and another non-canonical to be excluded is not quite clear. Modern Scripture scholars identify several criteria. First, and maybe most obviously, the writing had to be in line with mainstream beliefs. A writing claiming that Jesus was not divine just didn't fit. Second, there needed to be a sense that a specific text came from the first apostles, their initial successors, or in their line of apostolic succession. This is why some letters are "attributed to" an individual apostle or reputed to carry his aura of authority. Third, greater weight was given to writings that came from major, important, and influential churches. Fourth, the emperor Constantine, who favored Christianity in the first few decades of the fourth century, wanted there to be only one version of the Faith and so he played an important role in defining Christian Scripture to bolster that unifying expression of orthodox doctrine.

Constantine commissioned Eusebius, the bishop of Caesarea and a close adviser, to make fifty copies of a collection of texts to be used in the emperor's new capital of Constantinople, linking the Greek east with the Latin west at the same time. To do so, Eusebius decided on three batches of texts. First, he recognized those writings on which everyone agreed. These were the four familiar Gospels of Matthew, Mark, Luke, and John; Acts of the Apostles; thirteen Pauline letters plus 1 John and 1 Peter. Second, Eusebius then literally canonized epistles that had been disputed a bit, bringing them into the official fold: James, 2 Peter, Jude, 2 and 3 John, Hebrews, and Revelation. Third, he rejected certain texts, including gospels of Peter, Thomas, and Matthias; acts attributed to Andrew, Paul, and John; and an apocalypse of Peter. Eusebius also excluded some texts from this biblical canon that nevertheless remain authentic witnesses of the early Church and part of Church tradition: the Shepherd of Hermas, the *Didache*, and a pair letters attributed to a bishop in Rome named Clement.

As Christianity was becoming the only and official religion of the Roman Empire, a firm list quickly followed. Athanasius, an influential hero of Church doctrine and the bishop of Alexandria, in an Easter letter from about 367 accepted Eusebius' first two groups of writings, totaling twenty-seven books. Athanasius used the noun "canon" and the verb "to canonize" to demonstrate that he was giving official sanction to these writings, implicitly excluding others. In 393, a council of north African churches meeting in Augustine's diocese of Hippo listed the twenty-seven books of the New Testament that had by then become fairly set as the authoritative canon. Pope Innocent I agreed in 405, and provincial councils continued to list the twenty-seven books as well, such as at Carthage in 397 and 419.

About the same time, Jerome was assigned to translate this standard collection into Latin, which became the Vulgate edition that was the authoritative collection and translation for over a thousand years. In 1546, the Council of Trent declared again what were the forty-six Old Testament and twenty-seven New Testament books that it accepted as part of the official Catholic Bible.

But there were still discrepancies in the Old Testament, a situation that has implications for the modern Bibles on today's bookshelves and grows partially from the fact that we have very few original manuscripts or even fragments dating back to the Old and New Testament periods—certainly far fewer for the oldest Hebrew parts of the Old Testament. We can't point to any piece of papyrus, parchment, or paper and say that it was the original document written by the original author with his fingerprints still there. We can go back no further than the first century BC, just when the composition of the Old Testament was finishing up and the New Testament was still several decades in the future. This earliest source material makes up part of the electrifying find in 1948 of the Dead Sea Scrolls, but most of what we have of Jewish and Christian texts dates from early second century AD in bits and pieces, then longer segments and complete books dating to the third and fourth centuries.

From these sources in hand, now lost to us, certain Jews held to the short canon of thirty-nine books because they were in Hebrew. There are seven other books that Jews turn to as sacred and important, but they are not part of that Hebrew canon—in the same way that Christians count certain documents like the *Didache* as important, but not part of the Bible. These seven books are Tobit, Judith, 1 and 2 Maccabees, Wisdom, Baruch, and Ecclesiasticus (known as ben Sirach/ben Sira, and not to be confused with Ecclesiastes). There are also some chapters of Daniel and Esther that are in Christian Scripture, but not Jewish collections. These seven books are known as deutero-canonical books in Catholic circles and apocrypha to Protestants and Jews.

This moment would seem the right one to add that there are a fair number of modern translations, but a few dominate the market and therefore the conversation. Among English translations, you'll find some Bibles labeled as Protestant or Catholic versions. Translations are not new: we find English translations already in the 600s–700s, designed for commoners. In the Middle Ages, a group of scholars, including John Wycliffe, produced an English translation in the late fourteenth century. The British scholar William Tyndale, in exile in Germany, translated the New Testament from Greek into English and had it printed in 1525 in Cologne and Worms. Another English version was produced in Geneva in 1560. Both Tyndale's version and the *Geneva Bible* were brought to England. The *Geneva Bible* was especially popular among the everyday person. The Puritans who came to America and Shakespeare surely read it. Then came the stately *King James Bible* in 1611, which was considered authoritative and was revised between 1881 and 1885. On the Catholic side, an English translation of the Latin Vulgate appeared as the *Douay-Rheims Bible*, with the New Testament appearing in 1582 and the Old Testament following in 1609.

The *New Revised Standard Version* (NRSV) dating to 1990 is often called the Protestant Bible and owes its roots to the famous *King James Version* (KJV), through an intermediate revision in 1946–1952. Most Catholics use the *New American Bible* (NAB), which was published around 1970 and translated from original languages, with the New Testament translation revised in 1987. A newly revised edition of the NAB was published in 2010. Another Catholic version is the *New Jerusalem Bible* (NJB), published in 1966 and revised in 1985.

Interpreting Scripture

How was Scripture encountered by priests and people in the pews at the Church's local levels? Certainly, Paul's letters and Gospel accounts were read aloud at the first gatherings of the earliest Christians, many of whom were Jews and were used to hearing God's word in synagogue settings where rabbis preached on their sacred writings. Recall, for instance, the scene of Jesus in his hometown synagogue at Nazareth, reading a passage from Isaiah telling those gathered that the Spirit of the Lord was upon him, and then announcing its fulfillment in him standing right there (Luke 4:16–21, quoting Isaiah 61:1–2). The first clear reference we have to a Gospel reading is from Justin Martyr in the mid-second century. He attests that in Rome he heard in assembly a reading from apostles' "memoirs" or "memories" (likely Acts of the Apostles), though surely this had been a common practice for many decades by then. We know that at the *agape* meal and meeting of the earliest Christians, Paul's letters were read and indeed were surely written to be heard in just that setting and then to be exchanged from one assembly to another.

Once a priest or bishop read a passage, he would expound upon it and apply its message to the lives of his congregants. Perhaps in the first few decades of Christianity an elder was delegated for this task, as deacons are today. We also know that believers gathered in what we would call Bible study groups, but it wouldn't be long before some higher-end analysis was required, especially since doctrinal questions about Jesus' humanity and divinity were arising with different people turning to various scriptural passages to support their position and to refute other ideas.

We can trace in rough terms the development of different ways of reading and teaching Scripture over the centuries. The first commentators, whom we call the Fathers during the patristic period of the first few centuries of the Church's life, tended to write sermons and offer explanations that were both literal and allegorical, following a method that Jewish scholars and rabbis had used for several centuries already. A literal or historical explanation means they were discussing what really happened in Jesus' life: his words and deeds, his counsels and directions for a life of integrity, faith, and justice. Since Christian doctrine was developing at the same time, bishops especially also offered an allegorical or doctrinal approach: They taught what Christians were to believe and how they should act by using Scripture as a touchstone.

So, what preachers were trying to present was not only what had happened, but what it meant on a deeper level for the place, time, and situation of their listeners. This effort was sometimes contentious since it involved establishing orthodox faith and refuting what were being labeled, in contrast, as heretical ideas. But it was also an easier task once the canon was set. In fact, there is something of a chicken-and-egg situation at work here. The need to explain the Faith played a key role in deciding which versions of Scripture and particular books were to be included and excluded in the authoritative collection eventually codified as the New Testament which, as we've just seen, was pretty clear by the start of the fifth century.

Over time, as the challenge to be a Christian moved from the period of martyrdom in the Church's first three centuries to a longer medieval millennium of living the Faith across Europe, we find preachers, theologians, and bishops turning more often to a moralistic way of reading and preaching Scripture. Preachers used Scripture as a starting point, certainly, but their sermons tended more to be directed at giving advice to priests and parishioners on the best way to apply biblical lessons to their own diverse circumstances. This is known as the moral or tropological method: using Scripture to teach believers not so much what to believe as how to act based on that belief. It is the next logical step.

As the Middle Ages proceeded, and especially after universities increasingly became the centers of theological thinking starting in the twelfth century, more complex ways of studying Scripture developed. There was another method known as the mystical or anagogical way that pointed from this world to the next: based on Scripture, what could a Christian hope for not only in this life, but especially in the next? Medieval commentators glossed Scriptures, which means they literally wrote in the margins around the printed page or between the lines, inserting their comments directly by the spots in Scripture they were discussing. These glosses were so common and varied that scholars saw the need for an authoritative version, since obviously the diversity of glosses couldn't all agree in every detail. The major gloss, compiled in France in the middle of the twelfth century, was called simply *Glossa ordinaria*: the ordinary or common gloss. It took as its text Jerome's Latin Vulgate and became the most-used reference work among bishops and theologians in the Middle Ages, being copied in thousands of manuscripts in whole or part.

By the time of the Middle Ages, therefore, we find four standard ways of interpreting the Bible, frequently called the fourfold sense of Scripture. The literal sense was just that: what we're sure happened or what we can take at face value. The allegorical sense was especially applied to difficult passages and was sometimes known as the figurative sense, too. The moral or tropological sense indicated moral guidance or directives of just what the Christian way to act is. Finally, the anagogical sense looked to the time when the Church on earth would conclude and give way to the eternal kingdom of heaven. This approach was quite intellectual and even remote, with little popular appeal. At the same time, and despite the popularity and great achievement as well as considerable contribution of the *Glossa ordinaria*, we should say that as the Middle Ages progressed, Scripture started to take a bit of a back seat to theology. Especially in university circles, scholastic theologians used Scripture as a resource to back up their assertions as proof texts that sometimes removed the historical and literary context of a particular Bible verse or story.

This approach, which then and now can do damage to the full meaning of one word or sentence, was turned back as the Renaissance approached, with humanists taking up a special interest in the original languages and manuscripts of the Bible. They looked back behind Jerome's Latin Vulgate to the Hebrew and Greek of biblical people to return to the original sources. In Italy and Spain especially, where Christian scholars had contact with Jewish and Muslim source material that provided a link to early Church documents, schools arose that laid out different translations side by side with original languages—not unlike what had happened when the canon developed more than a thousand years earlier.

This linguistic or philological approach refreshed biblical study and gave it an immediacy it had lost. There were several important products of this humanistic reorientation of Bible study. One was a *Complutensian Polyglot Bible,* whose patron was Cardinal Francisco Ximénez de Cisneros. Produced at the University of Alcalá in 1514–1517, it won papal approval a few years later and was printed in the new book form and not in the older, slower, and more expensive handwritten manuscript fashion that was more susceptible to human error. It offered the Old Testament in three parallel columns of Hebrew, Greek, and Latin with the New Testament in two columns of Greek and Latin. Another great achievement was Erasmus' New Testament in Greek, published in 1516, followed by many volumes of the Fathers in Greek and Latin, all of which had been refreshed by the new concern to return to the original sources. Over in Germany, Martin Luther was engaged in much the same effort, though his goal was not just to go back to the original sources, but to produce a fresh and accessible German translation of the Bible into the everyday language of the people. He used Erasmus' fresh Greek New Testament as his text, rendering it into German in 1522; his German Old Testament, translated from Hebrew, appeared in 1534.

Scripture and Tradition

■ *Classic definitions and recent developments*

Of course, it was not just Luther's German Bible that is important for the development of the Church's encounter with Scripture, but his statements on how authoritative Scripture was, particularly when placed in relationship with Church Tradition. The questions were tangled together. Did Scripture or Tradition have higher authority? Who decides? And, who decides who decides—that is, on what basis is an authority authoritative: on the basis of Scripture and/or Tradition? It's a classic Catch-22, with questions and answers running in circles. Nevertheless, we must try to turn the circle into a straight line in order to understand the discussion of Scripture and Tradition as twin sources of revelation. We will try to see where that idea came from, how it was turned upside down and inside out during the turbulent and confusing sixteenth century, and where the Roman Catholic Church went after Luther.

The Protestant Reformation is often described with a series of alone statements: grace alone, faith alone, Scripture alone. It's just not that simple, especially when it comes to *sola scriptura*, because even Luther saw the need for scriptural explanations by informed people. In his own work, he relied on authoritative statements made by the Church's Fathers from the early chapters of Church history. Still, we can say generally that the Protestant position allowed most anyone to read and explain Scripture. Particularly in the sixteenth century, the Roman Catholic Church's hierarchy maintained that it should patrol scriptural interpretation and be the ultimate word on how a passage should be understood, while individual Christians were not permitted to make pronouncements on their own authority as baptized believers.

Moreover, Protestant churches rely more on Scripture itself than the accumulating body of Catholic pronouncements called Tradition. It was the Roman Catholic Church's position that Scripture contains what is called the deposit of revealed faith or revelation, but the precise content of that faith is not always clear because Scripture can be indirect. There are sometimes different versions of the same story, for instance, and a variety of literary genres must be interpreted a certain way. This is what the methodology of the fourfold senses of Scriptures tried to uncover.

Roman Catholic Tradition came from a variety of sources that leaders believed to be under the Holy Spirit's guidance: statements by the Fathers, creeds and decisions of general councils, some papal pronouncements. Bishops participated in this teaching authority and the preservation of authentic Tradition by grace of apostolic succession. Starting with the earliest council creeds and statements of faith, we find council Fathers and bishops pointing to Scripture as their north star, but specific scriptural passages needed explanation—or unpacking, to use a modern phrase. To use a very early Church example, a bishop named Irenaeus from Lyons late in the second century taught that Scripture and Tradition are yoked together, that they cannot exist apart from each other, and that they require authentic interpretation by those in the line of apostolic succession, which meant over the centuries the Church's body of bishops led by the pope.

It fell to the Council of Trent to state this position clearly since Protestant churches had challenged Roman Catholic authority, especially the role played by bishops and popes as final arbiters of what Scripture says. Throughout their deliberations and pronouncements, Trent's bishops noted that their decisions were based on Scripture and Tradition—not just Scripture—and on Scripture as they and only they authentically and ultimately interpreted the deposit of faith revealed in sacred writings. After affirming in 1546 just what books comprised the Old and New Testaments, Trent directed that a fresh translation of the Latin Vulgate appear. In doing so, in fact, Trent's bishops exercised and demonstrated their authority as the final word on the word of God. They also explained the integrated roles of Scripture and Tradition as two sources of revelation flowing from God. In 1965, Vatican II's main statement on Scripture, *Dei verbum*, reiterated the two sources of revelations—Scripture and Tradition—and the essential job of the Church's magisterium or teaching authority. Both Trent and Vatican II wanted to make sure that good scriptural interpretation reached the pews: this pair of councils mandated that priests preach every Sunday and feast day, which strikes us as obvious but wasn't always happening.

Between Trent in the sixteenth century and Vatican II in the twentieth century, biblical scholarship was transformed and expanded on a grand scale. We use the word "criticism" to describe new schools of methodology and interpretation, but we mean scholarly or academic exploration and not criticism in the sense of scolding or correcting. Several new schools emerged, starting particularly in the nineteenth century as part of a worldwide reappropriation of the ancient world through the new science of archaeology, which tried to find Homer's Troy, for example, and became fascinated with ancient Egypt and the Holy Land.

Once again, we find study of Scripture and Tradition, specifically as it related to the development of doctrine, closely intertwined. An influential German school focused on the history of doctrine called *Dogmengeschichte* and led by Adolf von Harnack (1851–1930) was fueled by the fast-moving advances in scriptural scholarship. On the Anglican and then Catholic side, John Henry Newman (1801–1890) traced how doctrine developed in the fourth century: Fathers took up topics and questions raised by Scripture, then expounded upon them to produce creeds that were grounded in Scripture but required explanation by bishops.

Catholic scholarship started slowly but picked up quite a head of steam as the twentieth century progressed. In 1893, Pope Leo XIII issued an encyclical called *Providentissimus Deus* that said the Bible cannot be discussed in the language of science, but he also established the Biblical Commission in 1902, put in place the steps that would lead to the Pontifical Biblical Institute, and opened the Vatican archives. In 1906, that Biblical Commission stated that all Catholics must believe Moses was the sole author of the Pentateuch, the first five books of the Bible, a position few scholars would hold then or now. At the same time, Leo wanted laypeople to read the Bible in approved vernacular translations. In 1943, Pope Pius XII issued *Divino Afflante Spiritu,* called by Scripture scholars the Magna Carta of their field, that significantly changed the tenor of the conversation. Pius XII gave free rein to Scripture scholarship by recognizing the variety of the Bible's literary genres, and by encouraging scholars and teachers to use all the tools of modern scholarship and methodologies. In *Dei verbum,* Vatican II singled out these methods as helpful.

The major school was historical criticism, which is closely related to form criticism or literary style. Modern scholars try to put the author of a specific biblical book in his historical place, time, and cultural context. What was his situation? What was his motivation in writing this book? Why did he choose this genre and not another? For whom did he write? What were this audience's concerns and situations? Textual or source criticism looks at the manuscripts themselves and tries to figure out which came first, which books drew on earlier versions, and which can be seen as closest to the starting point. It wonders about the process of oral tradition, which by its very nature leaves no written trace.

Even now, the Church continues to return to its scriptural sources through continuing biblical scholarship and Bible study groups in parishes. This has been, happily, much more of an ecumenical effort in recent years. With their concern for a return to the sources, Erasmus and Luther were practicing a shared form of textual or source criticism, even if they were on opposite sides of the Protestant-Catholic split at the time of its very birth. In the last century, biblical scholarship has exploded in part because doors were open in a number of academic fields between Catholic and Protestant scholars working together, many of whom developed personal friendships and professional alliances. This spirit of ecumenism and scholarly dialogue continues with the fact that, in the last fifty years, Protestants and Catholics have been involved in the translations and revisions of each other's Bibles. Scripture, which in Church history has served to divide Christians, is bringing them closer together again.

Discussion questions

- Did anything surprise you about the development of the canon?

- What has your experience with the Bible been, especially when faced with curious or confusing stories?

- What has your encounter been with other Christians who read the Bible differently than you?

- How might Catholics take up Bible study with as much enthusiasm and in such large numbers as their Protestant brothers and sisters?

- How could your understanding of the Bible grow deeper?

CHAPTER 3

Doctrine

WHAT CATHOLICS BELIEVE

At first, figuring God out

When we say that doctrine develops, we don't mean that a belief wasn't true or didn't exist before the Church made an official statement on a particular matter. For instance, Jesus was fully human and fully divine from the moment of his conception in Mary's womb, but the Church didn't formulate and agree on the words to describe this mystery until the councils of the fourth and fifth centuries came up with the creedal statements we repeat each Sunday when we say at Mass, "I believe in one God...he...was incarnate of the Virgin Mary, and became man." It's simply a matter of human beings in different centuries and changing contexts using a variety of languages to try to capture what they believe. Over time, the Church found even better ways to catch up to divine mysteries, but we must admit that they can never adequately be put into human words.

As the Church moved from groups of believers waiting for Jesus to return to a more structured association of communities across the Mediterranean basin, questions emerged. The early Church's first concern was explaining God as Father, Son, and Spirit, along with many related questions. How could three be one? How could Jesus be divine and human: was he half human and half divine? What was his relationship to his mother and Father? Was he two people: one human and one divine? Did the Spirit come from the Father or the Son—or Father and Son? Was one person in the Trinity lower than the other two?

Christianity's essential beliefs (*kerygma*) had to be passed along as the Faith spread. The essential facts of the Easter events—Jesus' death and resurrection—had to be explained to pagans who couldn't accept that God could die and return or that God could become human without losing divinity. These explanations varied in their accuracy, and so gradually bishops in different locations corresponded with each other to ask how each was dealing with this or that question or explanation. Doctrine developed from questions.

Let's look at several examples to see how this question-and-answer process occurred. One group of Christians wondered how God's three-ness in the Trinity related to God's one-ness as Father, as Son, and as Spirit. This question led to a series of positions, all of which were ultimately labeled heretical. One was called modal monarchianism: at any one time, God was never three but only one. God was Father (not Son or Spirit), and then Son (not Father or Spirit), and then Spirit (not Father or Son).

Another example is found in Adoptionism, which claimed the Father adopted the human Jesus and raised him to divinity, but the Son's divinity was inferior to the Father's. Arius, a priest in Alexandria in the early fourth century, believed Jesus was neither co-eternal with nor equal to the Father. As Son, Jesus had followed at a later date and had been made by the Father, so he was consequently some-how inferior to the Father, which linked with Adoptionism. Arius spoke about Jesus by saying there had been a time when Jesus had not existed. This position meant the Spirit was all the more made by Father (and/or Son) and inferior to both of them. Trouble arose when it came to salvation: if Jesus is not as fully God as the Father, then humans are not saved since only God can save.

In fact, this very process of struggling to explain mysteries is how statements of orthodoxy and heresy developed. For instance, a believer named Marcion (ca. 85–160) misunderstood Jesus' existence as man and God because he could not understand how evil could exist in the world—a perennial question. Marcion, whom we met in the chapter on Scripture, believed there were two Gods (dualism): one God was good (the Father of Jesus) and the other was bad. The bad god created the world, including evil. Marcion believed Jesus could not have truly been a man because the world and material objects were evil. Therefore, Jesus had not really been born of a woman, had not truly died, and did not in fact come back from the dead—which again created obvious problems for salvation history.

With all of these questions and answers competing with each

other, Church leaders had to come together and make definitive statements. But Christians couldn't do this while Christianity remained illegal under the pagan Roman emperors. When the Roman emperor Constantine tolerated Christianity starting in 313, however, bishops and thinkers could meet openly to settle questions. Constantine himself wanted one clear version of Christianity, so he oversaw a meeting that became the first of the Church's twenty-one general councils. It met in Nicaea, in modern-day Turkey, in 325. There, a deacon named Athanasius refuted Arius. Asked how the Son is equal to the Father, Athanasius replied that it was like the sight of two eyes. The bishops agreed to state precisely that Jesus is begotten, not made and is one in being with the Father (the key Greek word denoting *in being with* is rendered in English letters as *homo-ousious*) as well as the Father's equal. The second general council, which met at Constantinople (today's Istanbul) in 381 applied the same concept to the Holy Spirit, saying that it, too, was of the same being as Father and Son; that Father, Son, and Spirit are co-eternal; and all three persons of the Trinity are equal. There was never a time, in other words, when the Spirit or Son were not in equal co-existence with the Father.

New answers created more questions, which in turn led to competing ideas that had to be sifted by the Church's authorities. A monk named Nestor (ca. 381–451), taught that Mary had been the mother of the human Jesus, but not the mother of God. Others who followed him claimed that Jesus had been two separate persons, one human (the son of Mary) and one divine (the son of God)—the catch phrase was other and other—which produced even more questions: was Jesus human sometimes and God at other times? Again, a council helped: Ephesus in 431 declared Nestorianism a heresy and stated clearly that Jesus has two natures (human and divine) joined in one person by a hypostatic union. Mary was indeed the mother of God (*theotokos*).

Still, doctrinal issues kept arising: monophysitism (one nature) held that Jesus' divine nature swallowed his human nature. This position had roots dating back about a hundred years, when a theologian named Apollinaris had fought Arianism by overemphasizing Jesus' divinity. While Arius had said Jesus was never divine, Apollinaris claimed Jesus was so divine that his divinity overtook his humanity. It took the fourth general council, Chalcedon in 451, to explain that God's divinity took humanity upon itself without either the divine or the human nature canceling the other out. Jesus is one person with two natures: human and divine. Mary is indeed the mother of God. The Trinity is made up of three persons—Father, Son, and Spirit—each of whom is co-equal, co-eternal, and of the same being with the other.

After the flurry of activity in the first four general councils, doctrinal questions kept coming. A second council of Constantinople met in 553 to reiterate that Nestorianism and monophysitism were heresies. Constantinople II reaffirmed the hypostatic union and all prior conciliar teachings on the Trinity, Christology, and Mary. Now that doctrine on these matters had been settled, the bishops stressed that anyone holding other positions, teaching them, or permitting others to hold or teach them should be condemned. But a final question still arose: how many wills did Jesus have? Preliminary discussions were held throughout the spreading world of Christianity—as far away as England—and opinions were gathered for discussion at the council. Constantinople III in 680–681 decided against the monothelitists who taught that Jesus had only one will.

The bishops declared that Jesus' human nature had one will and his divine nature had another will. Each did not cancel the other out.

Medieval and Reformation methods
■ *New paths to old questions*

Medieval theologians helped doctrine develop because of a new way of doing theology called scholastic theology. The medieval centuries were a period of cataloging, synthesizing, analyzing, and presenting doctrine in the most coherent, organized, systematic, and technical way yet seen in Church history. Scholastic theology was very different than monastic theology, which had dominated for about a millennium. Monastic theology had been fairly conservative, spiritual, and grounded in Scripture. Monastic theology addressed the will more than the intellect and readily deferred to mystery in a search for God within the individual human being. On the other hand, scholastic theology was more aggressive, assertive, inquisitive, and speculative, sometimes to a fault. It gave a greater role to human reason and logic, but was also very closely concerned with the most practical pastoral issues: questions concerning marriage make up some of the earliest work in doctrine and canon law that scholastic theologians tackled.

The first significant move away from monastic theology's approach came with Anselm of Canterbury (ca. 1033–1109), who in *Cur Deus Homo* (Why God Became Man) set out to prove that God exists. Anselm sought to demonstrate why God had to become human in order to save human beings—a clear desire to understand the integral connection between God and human beings that is so key to the incarnation. Anselm started from a position of faith in order to understand doctrine. In Latin, this is the famous phrase *fides quaerens intellectum*: faith seeking understanding. Abelard (1079–1142) added to this methodology more aggressively by lining up contradictory statements of doctrine and asking which was correct in his appropriately titled treatise *Sic et Non* (Yes and No). As he put it, "By doubting, we come to inquiry. Through inquiring, we perceive the truth." Abelard's goal was to create a synthesis of confusing, competing, and contradictory theological statements.

Abelard's work was in the same spirit as an influential law collection by Gratian that appeared in 1140. Usually called by the shorthand name of *Decretum*, its full title makes the practical point of scholastic theology much more clearly: *A Concordance of Discordant Canons*. Gratian took a legal question, ran through all the decisions and comments he could find on that question, listed their strengths and weaknesses, tried to reconcile their contradictions, and then made a definitive statement of what Church law should be. It was a collection that became the foundation of canon law.

Doctrine and Church law needed just this kind of tune-up after more than a thousand years of thinking, arguing, speculating, deciding, raising new questions, letting some answers sit, and revisiting old ideas with fresh words and concepts. Abelard and Gratian's method was quickly codified in formal steps of reasoning that were applied to doctrinal issues. First, a theologian raised a question, for instance, whether (*utrum*) angels had bodies. Then, he listed and explained the arguments, reasons, and precedents against this position by stating "it does not seem that…" (*videtur quod non…*). Next, he deliberately took the exact opposite stance: "but against this…" (*sed contra est…*). Next, he made a decision about the two prior steps, reconciled opposing ideas, and declared his position: "I respond that…" (*respondeo*). Finally, he listed his responses to any further objections that he thought might be raised against his position: "against the first point...and the second point..." (*ad primum...ad secundum...*). It wasn't long before questions were gathered together by theme and new genres appeared to discuss doctrine: for example, a *summa* was a large collection that treated a subject comprehensively (Eucharist, other sacraments, marriage, morality, the Trinity), while a *quodlibet* was a short opinion on a particular matter, typically a controversial contemporary debate.

Of course, Thomas Aquinas (ca. 1225–1274) is the superstar of medieval scholastic theology. Like his colleagues, he benefited from the revival of the study of Aristotle's thoughts on politics, logic, and ethics, which had been preserved by Muslims, Christians, and Jews. Across the Middle East and north Africa, Muslims had translated Greek sources into Arabic; in Spain, some of these Arabic sources were in turn translated into Hebrew and Latin. Because of trading contacts with Muslims in the Mediterranean, this material began to have a strong impact in Spain, Sicily, and Italy. Aquinas' *Summa Theologiae* is the most-well known attempt to reconcile the Church's traditional writings with this rediscovered Greek vocabulary, philosophy, and principles, but there were many *summae* written during the Middle Ages. He was not afraid to apply pagan principles to Christian doctrine, since he had such confidence in Catholic truth, nor did he think we should fear where our intellects and reason would take us. God, Aquinas knew, was ultimately a mystery beyond human genius—even his own: after he had a heavenly vision, he tried to destroy everything he'd written about doctrine.

The late medieval period was one where the negative aspects of scholasticism dominated doctrinal discussions. But even before Martin Luther posted his *Ninety-Five Theses* in 1517, a significant number of bishops, theologians, professors, and university leaders were complaining that doctrine had become divorced from pastoral, practical consequences. Many theologians were spending too much time away from the essentials of preaching, teaching, and spreading the Faith. Instead, they argued about tiny details in a kind of parlor game to show off how smart they were. Scholastic theology had devolved into cold lists of reasons why a position was right or wrong and was missing the purpose of moral guidance. Because doctrine had lost its way, humanists like Erasmus (ca. 1466–1536), along with Luther and other Protestant reformers, asked fundamental questions, just as the early Church had done. What were the primary texts and languages on which doctrine had been constructed? What was the point of certain Church beliefs and actions? Had some of the original meanings and intents of doctrine been lost in the later Middle Ages? What were the moral implications of doctrine? What is Jesus' role in salvation? What is the human's place in the world, in salvation, and in relationship with God? What is the authority of Scripture? Who judges doctrine?

Protestant and Catholic answers to these questions produced competing theologies, controversies, and debates that played out in public meetings and in a kind of pamphlet literature in the early decades of printing and publishing. Led by Martin Luther and John Calvin, the sixteenth-century Protestants saw many elements of the Catholic theological, sacramental, devotional, and legal systems as additions that came after the New Testament and early Church. Luther felt that these additions were not authentic developments, and so he sought a return to the first few centuries of Christianity before Constantine favored the Church with protection and patronage in the early fourth century. In terms of Church structure, Protestants identified in the early Church a horizontal arrangement of shared power that they aimed to adopt in their own place and time—in essence, establishing a different kind of ecclesiology that was more decentralized and local. These perspectives deleted years of doctrinal developments that were part of Catholicism's organic tradition, legitimate growth, and hierarchical structures.

The combination of Catholic humanism and Protestant challenge created the need for greater clarity and synthesis about just what Catholic doctrine was. The Council of Trent (1545–1563) answered these questions, producing a kind of response-reaction to doctrinal development that reminds us of the question-and-answer cycle of the first general councils concerning Christology, Trinitarian theology, and Mariology. Scholars call this development positive theology, which was the older, original scholastic theology stripped of the silliness of late medieval scholasticism. Positive theology focused on explaining Roman Catholic doctrine versus Protestant doctrines (specifically about Scripture, tradition, and the sacraments) both in terms of the original sources and legitimate development. They tried to avoid scholasticism and make statements that were clear, pastorally oriented, and comprehensible.

Trent reemphasized the importance of Scripture and its right interpretation by qualified authorities. The Fathers at Trent stated that Tradition (the teachings of the Fathers, conciliar and papal statements, creeds, and other authoritative decisions) partnered with Scripture as the twin poles of Church authority and doctrinal truth, especially when it came to the key questions of grace and justification that had been raised by Luther. He had strongly emphasized God's role in salvation and did not see any inherent merit in human action alone when it came to salvation. For him, the Catholic system of sacraments and indulgences was not only tainted by excess, but largely unnecessary when it came to salvation. Calvin had gone further by teaching that, from the moment of their creation, humans are destined to heaven or hell (double predestination). As for the related idea of original sin, there was a variety of Protestant ideas, most of which reached back to the fourth-century ideas of Pelagius, whose idea that Adam's sin stained only himself was declared a heresy and was fought back by Augustine. Likewise, some Protestants taught that Adam's sin tainted only himself while others went a little beyond that to say that he also set a bad example for others, although he did not pass original sin along to the rest of the human race.

Trent reaffirmed the need for human action and the role of free will while recognizing Jesus' essential and indispensable role in salvation. The council rejected predestination and stated that Adam's sin was transmitted to all other human beings. We are therefore born with original sin that must be wiped clean through baptism, a sacrament that makes a real change in a person's life and is not simply a symbolic introduction to Christianity.

The bishops declared clearly what the seven sacraments were and explained why they were sacraments. They explained all of the sacraments, but especially noted that the Eucharist is the Real Presence of Jesus that occurs during a process called transubstantiation, a scholastic word that had first been used at a general council by Lateran IV in 1215. This word is a good example of how scholastic theology's categories and vocabulary trickled up into official doctrine. This scholastic word allowed the Church to explain more precisely how the bread and wine are truly, completely, and permanently transformed into Jesus' real Body and Blood, although the bread and wine appear to remain. This teaching stood against a variety of Protestant beliefs about the "Lord's Supper," as it was commonly called in Protestant theology, which included consubstantiation (bread and wine remain and co-exist with Jesus' Body and Blood) and the idea of memorial alone, in which the bread and wine never change at all and only symbolize Jesus' Body and Blood.

Once Catholic doctrine had been reaffirmed and restated, apologists spread these teachings, sometimes in a combative or controversial way. On the Catholic side, the strongest example of this approach comes from the Jesuit Robert Bellarmine (1542–1621). His work *The Controversies* was a kind of Catholic textbook that was used to refute Protestant doctrines. His catechism, translated into more than sixty languages, was carried by missionaries around the globe until the twentieth century. More gently, other theologians, particularly in Spain and in the territories that would be called South and Latin America, tried to recapture the pastoral aspects of scholastic theology and humanism. Theologians and catechists turned to Scripture, Church history, canon law, and the councils to explain what authentic Catholic doctrine is and how it developed legitimately over time. Study of doctrine was also emphasized: the Jesuit program of study called the *Ratio Studiorum* mandated that every Jesuit school have a library budget. Peter Canisius (1521–1597), a Jesuit who worked hard in Germany to reclaim areas to Catholicism, declared bluntly that he would rather have a school without a Church than without a library. Doctrine was back on track.

Living doctrine

In the centuries after the Council of Trent finished its sessions in 1563, the Church devoted her energy to promoting its agenda of revitalizing catechism and of clarifying doctrine in light of competing Protestant theology. This effort resulted not in new doctrine developing, but in an emphasis on positive theology, moral theology, and apologetics (sometimes called controversial theology) designed to describe and defend Catholic doctrine. Greater attention was paid to explaining and proselytizing than to expanding doctrine. Demonstrations and presentations of dogma appeared more frequently than discussions, in part because Catholics were still competing with Protestants.

Moral theology had typically been integrated with other doctrines, but in this period treatises and catechetics were more directly focused on giving moral guidance and direction so people would know how to be Christian in accordance with Catholic doctrine. What was the best way to live what you believe? It's not that anything new was said, but the way morality was presented was fresher, clearer, easier to understand, and set apart from other branches of theology. As a result of these directions and goals—as well as of slowly increasing literacy rates—Catholic doctrine began to appear more frequently than ever before in encyclopedias, catechisms, manuals, and lists of proof texts that stated what a Catholic doctrine was and where the Church's teachings came from: Scripture, conciliar statements, and theological treatises. Books and pamphlets, particularly on moral theology, were written in a style and at a level aimed especially for the European masses and the indigenous populations that missionaries met in the Far East and the Americas. Above all, the Church's authority to teach doctrine, recognize error, and regulate conduct was affirmed repeatedly.

There were, however, two related Catholic doctrinal movements that veered into heresy in this period: Jansenism and Quietism. Both returned to long-standing questions: What is the human person's relationship with God? Where did grace and free will come into play within that relationship? Jansenism once again drew on Augustine's pessimism that said people tended to act poorly when motivated by lust and greed. Jansenism laid too great an emphasis on the sinfulness of human beings. Following a bishop and theologian named Cornelius Jansen (1585–1638) and his book *Augustinus,* published posthumously in 1640, Jansenists believed human beings had been born with justice, but lost it in the Fall. Christ restored that justice and therefore effected our redemption, but remarkably Jansen held that this action was still not enough for salvation. People needed additional grace to fight their evil tendencies; not everyone gets this extra grace from God. Jansen was not a Calvinist, however, because he believed humans who receive this grace must cooperate with God through their good works. But Jansen did come close to predestination in his notion of the elect and non-elect, which denied the Catholic doctrine that everyone can be saved.

Jesuit scholastic humanists were also writing on these topics, but they took a more optimistic approach and were sometimes accused by the Jansenists of being too lax when it came to pronouncing on human sin and culpability in moral theology. In response, the Jesuits labeled the Jansenists as rigorists. The Jesuits stressed the Catholic doctrine that Christ provided sufficient grace through his passion for humanity's redemption. Apart from differences in fundamental theology, in practical terms the conflict between Jesuits and Jansenists might come down to this: if a person thought he might have sinned, the Jesuit would allow him to receive the Eucharist, but the Jansenist would forbid receiving. It should come as no surprise that two popes, Innocent X in 1653 and Clement XI in 1713, condemned Jansenism.

Quietism saw human beings as extremely passive in their relationship with God and approached Protestant doctrine by denying that good works played an important role in a human being's salvation. Quietists recommended long periods of very quiet prayer in which Christians abandoned themselves to God and waited passively to receive insight or revelations. Quietism also deemphasized the role of the intellect in contemplating God. It wasn't long before Quietists were rejecting good works, traditional devotions, and even some sacraments—yet another reason they were labeled as Protestants since the task of reiterating what is and isn't Catholic doctrine is the most marked characteristic of the early modern age.

As we turn to the most recent one hundred fifty years or so of Church history, we witness quite a combination of developments: a revival of traditional scholasticism, the introduction of new methods of doing theology, and some new ideas that have met with mixed responses. This period of Church history has seen an intense and varied period of reexamined and revitalized theology, often based on scientific methods being applied to doctrine, Church history, liturgy, and Scripture—what is often loosely placed under the large umbrella phrase *nouvelle théologie*. We've had three major teachings in the modern Church: the doctrine of the Immaculate Conception (1854), the infallibility of the pope's teaching authority (1870), and the assumption (1950). Beyond these major statements, modernity has been one of the richest periods of theology since the Church's first few centuries.

One of the most significant developments was the revival of scholasticism, especially as represented by Thomas Aquinas. We generally call this movement neo-scholasticism, the neo-scholastic revival, or neo-Thomism. The big push came with Pope Leo XIII's encyclical *Aeterni Patris* (1879), which restored scholastic theology in seminaries. The pope also established the Roman Academy of Saint Thomas and another study center devoted to Aquinas in Louvain. He ordered that Aquinas' texts be reedited and declared Aquinas the patron saint of Catholic education. Journals in diverse languages soon focused on Aquinas, with many articles applying the scholastic method to modern questions of philosophy and doctrine. The next pope, Pius X, required that Aquinas' *Summa Theologiae* be the principal theology textbook in all schools, specifically seminaries, that gave pontifical decrees.

Although we have been talking for some time already about the development of doctrine, the theologian who spoke most eloquently about this idea lived at the dawn of modernity. John Henry Newman (1801–1890) reached back to the fourth century Arian controversies to remind Christians that doctrinal definitions will always fall short of God's reality. No phrase, no creed, no treatise can capture the essence of revelation, so he reminded Catholics to beware of intellectual arrogance that put reason ahead of revelation, subjective knowledge before objective truth, and a man or woman ahead of God. Newman searched the history of doctrine for the continuity of religious principles that do not change, even if the words used to describe doctrines had evolved. He saw Tradition as something that lived and breathed, but that did not change in its essential truth. In a sermon he gave in 1839 on "Faith and Reason, Contrasted as Habits of the Mind," Newman explained that faith and reason are very different approaches to knowledge and truth. Speaking in a very scholastic style (proposition, arguments against faith and then in support of faith, objections, resolution of contradictions), Newman concluded that while religious assent depends to a certain degree on the probability of a truth and its logic, scientific proof can never lead the heart to real faith. In this way, Newman synthesized the medieval and early modern tension between faith and intellect, pointing the way to a modern theology that embraced new methods while keeping faith and mystery in a central position.

The modern Church, indeed, witnessed theology reborn with new methodologies. As the nineteenth century progressed and crossed into the twentieth, Protestant and Catholic scholars and theologians, especially in France and Germany, employed Church history, archaeology, and textual analysis of Scripture and many other documents to revisit doctrine and enhance Christian teachings with greater clarity, accuracy, and freshness. They saw revelation as something ongoing and dynamic, yet always in dialogue with Tradition. Church history especially helped theologians and bishops before, during, and after Vatican II to renew liturgy, prayer, spirituality, and ecclesiology by returning these areas to the Church's earliest centuries to find the most original and authentic expressions of Christian life, but then to update them to the modern world.

The modern age has offered not so much new doctrines as new ways of looking at traditional beliefs. Vatican II (1962–1965) was not a doctrinal council like Nicaea I or Trent, but a pastoral council that gave shape and authority to various shifts in theology that had been brewing for over a century. These shifts asked us to look again at key parts of Catholicism, but to use new scholarly and pastoral methods and ideas that reached a certain critical mass at the council and afterward. They also pressed Catholics to understand how doctrine must be applied in practical ways in their families, communities, and workplaces—to engage the world and not shrink from it. As a result, we have had renewed theologies of the laity (single, married, parenthood), of the permanent diaconate, of ecclesiology, and of the very idea of what we mean by the word "vocation." We have also had theologies that have drawn criticism from the Church's authorities, such as Pope John Paul II's rejection of some of the methods of liberation theology from Latin and South America. Surely, much more work needs to be done, particularly on theologies that wake up our understanding, appreciation, and celebration of confirmation and penance, as well as the essential role of women. As always, Catholics must remember that doctrine's development must be aligned with Church history, Tradition, and authority if it is to be judged as an authentic expression of truth, while recognizing that no statement of doctrine can ever fully capture the essence of that mysterious truth.

Discussion questions

- Were you surprised to find that doctrine developed?

- Do you have a different understanding of heresy now that you see the role it played?

- Where do you think the Church stands today in terms of its ability to communicate her teachings to young people and the non-Catholic world?

- The doctrines regarding Jesus Christ, the Trinity, and Mary are interrelated. What are the extreme positions that need to be avoided in each of the teachings?

- What fields of theology do you think need to be emphasized more today? Do you think a monastic approach, a scholastic approach, or some combination or new type of method would help make theology more relevant to people's lives today?

CHAPTER 4

Mass

HOW CATHOLICS CELEBRATE SUNDAY

Making Sunday

The most important thing to remember about the earliest Christians is that they were mostly Jews: it's natural that their liturgies developed from Jewish sources. The Last Supper may have been a Jewish seder or something like it, so it didn't take long for the first Christians to gradually adapt Jewish rituals to their new faith in Jesus Christ as the Son of God. In the first few centuries of Christianity, what we call the Mass developed slowly in the context of a shared meal on the Jewish sabbath of Friday night, but gradually moved away from the meal into its own liturgical service on Sunday mornings to mark the day of Jesus' resurrection.

In the Jewish ritual that Jesus' first followers would have practiced for most of their lives, bread and wine were blessed separately and probably at the beginning of a meal. This is what the earliest Christians did for the few years right after Jesus' death and resurrection. But by the 40s AD, a little more than a decade later, it appears that bread and wine were blessed together at the end of a fellowship meal, which was called an *agape*. Moving the blessing ritual to the end of the meal led to something of a separation of the Eucharist (from the Greek word for the act of giving thanks) from the *agape*, which led over time to a complete separation of the two events: a meal and a Eucharist. In today's Mass, there's a vestige of the union of Eucharist and *agape*: the offertory represents the time when people would bring food and drink to the combined events.

This separation may have occurred because the *agape* had become the scene of a little too much drinking, divisions, and the unfair distribution of food so that some Christians even went hungry. Paul chastised the Corinthians for such scandalous behavior at their gatherings, which should have been the occasion for fellowship and forgiveness, in the 50s AD (1 Corinthians 11:17–22). By the end of the first century and the beginning of the second, the Eucharist and the *agape* had pulled apart. The Eucharist moved to Sunday morning and the meal to Saturday or Sunday evening, but it disappeared entirely by the early fourth century, probably because Christians could gather more freely and any time they wanted after Constantine favored Christianity about that time.

Because the Eucharist was separated from the *agape*, some things were lost: talking, sharing news, directions from leaders, reading of Paul's letters or passages from the Gospels, singing—everything that makes a meal a celebration. Following Jewish examples from synagogue services, Christians on Saturday mornings gathered for a pair of readings from Scripture, a sermon, prayers for aid, and songs. It wasn't long before this Saturday morning service (what we now call the Liturgy of the Word) was combined with Sunday morning's Liturgy of the Eucharist. Probably within a century after Jesus' time on earth, but surely by the early 200s, we can find a Mass fairly close in structure to our own experience.

All of these gatherings were celebrated in Greek, which was the language of the people, but we find in the few records we have a certain diversity. At the Word liturgy, the Eucharist, and the *agape*, there was probably a head table, perhaps raised, at which sat the presider, who was usually the man we today call the bishop. Different leaders, however, conducted their services using variations of prayers, readings, and blessings because formulaic prayers and standard versions of Scripture were not yet codified. There was some freedom in the wording of prayers, but surely an oral culture that handed important words down by mouth made certain that the key words of the Eucharist were as close to uniform as possible. Moreover, some rituals occurred at different times during the liturgy. Christians exchanged the kiss of peace after the intercessions and before the offertory until the fifth century, when the kiss was moved to the Eucharist. During the 300s in north Africa and Rome, Christians kissed after the eucharistic prayer. We know, too, that Christians received the Eucharist not on their tongues, but in their hands.

By the early third century, however, leaders were urging greater precision in liturgical language and practice, which was important since how Christians pray must match what doctrines they believe. A Christian leader named Hippolytus wrote a manual called *Apostolic Tradition* about 225, with texts to be used by everyone in their liturgies. His earliest version of the eucharistic prayers with which we are familiar was still in Greek at this point, and it had the intended effect of making the vocabulary of the Eucharist more standard and less diverse. By the early 200s, the liturgies in Rome were in Latin, and by the late 300s, Latin was more common everywhere. The result was that both the Bible, under Jerome's Vulgate translation, and liturgical services took on a more formal, standard, and literary tone.

The Mass also developed its own place and time. In 321, the Roman Emperor Constantine—who by this time was favoring Christianity—made Sunday a day of rest. The Lord's Day was now a legal day off every week, but Christians had been gathering for over 200 years already on that day of Jesus' resurrection. Where did they gather? Within weeks or months after Jesus' resurrection, Jews met in their synagogues and homes—later called house churches—to talk about Jesus. Once the Romans leveled Jerusalem and scattered the Jews into exile in 70 AD, these house churches sprang up with growing frequency around the Mediterranean lands, although they had begun to do so even before Jerusalem fell. As Christianity pulled away from Judaism, the house churches replaced the synagogues.

After the Roman Empire declined through the fifth century, the Mass and other liturgies grew more standardized, largely through the efforts of the popes and his theologians in Rome, who wanted to be sure that all Christians were literally on the same page when celebrating the Eucharist. Because popes were directing missionaries to go into central Europe and spread the Faith to pagans while defending it against heretics, there was a need for a solid and standard way of saying Mass to unify the growing Church. The way to achieve this goal of uniformity was to establish certain texts as the authentic collections of prayers, readings, and rituals that everyone was to follow in order to say Mass properly. Most of these texts dealt with the elaborate liturgies as they were celebrated by popes and bishops, not the simple Mass celebrated by a priest in a small parish. Still, these Roman collections served as a starting point and guide, with the hope that a standard liturgy would eventually trickle down into the parishes and unite Christians spread throughout Europe. In fact, the Synod of Whitby held in 664 mandated that all Christians in the British Isles, and especially the Irish who were dating Easter according to a formula different than Rome's, had to adopt Roman liturgical rites.

The most important collections were called *Sacramentaries*, which were gathered together under the names of several popes, including Leo I (440–461), Gelasius I (492–496), and Gregory I (590–604). These popes did not have a hand in the *Sacramentaries* that bore their names, but the identification of their names lent prestige and authenticity to the collections, which began to appear in the middle of the 500s. These *Sacramentaries* included prayers and blessings said on feasts or during particular liturgical seasons such as Lent and Advent, the prayers said over the gifts of bread and wine, the prayers of consecration, and prayers said before and after Communion.

Groups of readings for the Mass were collected in *Lectionaries*. At first, these collections held only the beginning (*incipit*) and ending (*explicit*) words of the passages to be read, which the priest could use to find the complete selection in his Bible. Later, the full texts of the passages were published in the *Lectionaries*. Some *Lectionaries* contained only Paul's letters or the Gospels. Collections of hymns and chanted parts of the Mass called antiphonaries followed. They included the entrance hymn, the *Kyrie*, the Gloria, the Gradual (what we call the responsorial psalm), the *Credo*, the *Sanctus*, the *Agnus Dei*, and the closing statement *Ite, missa est* ("Go, the Mass is ended."). Sample homilies, often drawn from the Fathers, were gathered in homilaries. To make sure that the Mass was conducted properly, directions were written in red ink—from which we get the word rubric—in all of these collections so the Mass celebrant would know what to do when. Sometimes there were books of nothing but rubrics. These books or directions were often used by a master of ceremonies and were called *ordines*.

What effect did these collections have on the Mass? During the second part of the first millennium of Christianity, we see liturgies becoming more uniform in the most essential parts of the Mass, such as the consecration, although local variety still existed for certain rituals. Most especially, we see the Roman way of celebrating Mass spreading to central Europe and over to modern-day Spain and Portugal. Christianity found a base north of Rome in the imperial courts of Pepin III (751–768), his son Charlemagne (768–814), and Charlemagne's son Louis the Pious (814–840), all of whom pumped money and patronage into libraries and study centers where theology and liturgy were codified, copied, and disseminated with papal approval and cooperation.

While the Mass had become more austere, stately, and formal, there was also change and growth. During the seventh century, important additions were made to the Mass. These were aspects of liturgies as they were celebrated in different parts of Christianity that gradually came to be included by everyone, such as the *Kyrie*, the *Agnus Dei*, and the breaking of the host. The creed had been used during baptisms, but not always Masses. Under Charlemagne, the creed was added after the Gospel. From his court in northern Europe, this introduction of the creed into the Mass went to Rome, an example of an aspect of the Mass being introduced from Christianity's periphery to her center in Rome and then, from Rome, to the rest of the Church.

We may step back to observe that these developments had positive and negative aspects. Certainly structure and uniformity were essential to a faith that must celebrate the Mass in substantially the same way and believe the same things theologically. But it also appears that there was a healthy balance of uniformity in essentials and diversity in local devotions or practices, which allowed missionaries on Europe's frontiers to bring new believers into the Faith without alienating them. Celtic and German songs were transformed into Christian hymns, for instance. As much as Charlemagne wanted liturgical uniformity with Rome, he found that local customs were not included in the Roman Mass collections and set his favorite scholar Alcuin (ca. 735–804) to the task of gathering and adding them for his local bishops and priests.

At the same time, parishioners were gradually moving away from participating in the liturgy to watching it happen. Latin was no longer the vernacular language, but it remained the liturgical language, so Christians did not always understand what was being spoken at the altar. This led liturgists, in turn, to introduce symbolic dramatizations such as entrance and Gospel processions, multiple incensations, and anointings during episcopal and royal consecrations. These dramatizations included the parishioners in the Mass, but sometimes distracted them from the centrality of the consecration. Over time, extra-liturgical practices began to attract more of their attention than the Mass did, which leads us to the Middle Ages.

Medieval Mass and Reformation reforms

The Middle Ages saw a variety of devotional practices that in some cases supported and at other times diverted attention away from the Mass. While the Middle Ages witnessed a tremendous upsurge in popular devotions, the central act of people's faith was not always the Mass. Medieval Christians loved a party, and there were many feast days devoted to local saints and Mary with processions, plays, and fairs. Many of these allowed Christians to exercise their devotions, but they did not always include Mass in that devotion. There were several reasons for this development, but it was the rise of individual Masses that dominates this part of Church history.

During the medieval period, there was a dramatic increase in the number of Masses said by individual priests with no one except a single altar server in attendance. This did not happen because Christians abandoned the Mass, however. In fact, quite the opposite was true: there was such faith that a Mass said for a particular purpose—especially to help someone's soul graduate from purgatory to heaven—that people believed the more Masses were directed to their intention, the better the chance that the intention would be fulfilled. This motivation led people to endow churches and especially monasteries with gifts of money so Masses could be said for one specific purpose: typically, to pray for your soul or the soul of a family member (perhaps even in perpetuity) to make sure their sins were forgiven and they were allowed to enter heaven. Despite the laudable faith behind this motivation, the result was that the Mass began to lose several elements that were extremely important: the active participation of the faithful and the exercise of the Mass as a communal—as opposed to an individual—celebration.

These individual Masses were called private Masses, but were also known as dry or read Masses because they were often stripped to the bare essentials. There were no hymns, no responses from a congregation (which frequently was not even present), no incensations, and no interaction between priest and people, although there was an increase in prayers said by the priest alone. The kiss of peace disappeared among the people. If more than one priest was present, they shared the kiss of peace among themselves alone or simply kissed a plate or paten (on which the Eucharist would rest) and passed it along to the next priest. It's not surprising that people received holy Communion at Mass rarely. When they did, they now received on the tongue, not in the hand, and the chalice was given only to royalty or aristocracy, if at all. So infrequent was receiving Communion that the Fourth Lateran Council in 1215 had to order Christians to confess their sins and receive the Eucharist once a year, which came to be known as the Easter duty.

This did not mean, however, that people lost faith in the Eucharist. There's a great deal of evidence to the contrary: there was such a reverence for the Eucharist that people did not think they measured up to receiving Communion more than once a year. We know of the esteem for the Eucharist from two main sources. First, elevations of the Eucharist became important moments in the Mass. When many Masses were being said in side-by-side altars set along the main bodies of large Churches and basilicas, parishioners would move from one altar to the next, sometimes shouting "Higher" at the elevation so they could see the Eucharist. Masses were sometimes begun at five-minute intervals just so people could move from one altar to the next when they heard the altar server ring a little bell to signal the next elevation. Second, *Corpus Christi* processions were wildly popular during the Middle Ages, with elaborate floats and celebrations marking the movement of the Eucharist, displayed in a monstrance, through the town square. While some of this—along with morality and passion plays, veneration of relics, saints' feasts, and rosaries—surely at times led to excesses of devotion that may have been devoid of complete understanding of the Real Presence and other theological points, it cannot be denied that there was real faith and reverence for the Eucharist and the faith behind these actions.

At the same time, the Masses and rituals of Holy Week became more elaborate, which also indicated religious devotion even if people were not receiving Communion. Many of these rituals grew because of the rising number of pilgrims and crusaders who had spent time in the Holy Land and witnessed there the intricate Holy Week liturgies celebrated at the very places where Jesus suffered, died, was buried, and rose from the dead. They brought these memories home with them and the clergy who traveled to Bethlehem and Jerusalem were in a position to incorporate the Holy Land liturgies into European settings. In an increasing number of places in Europe, there was a procession on Palm Sunday, the public washing of feet on Holy Thursday, the chanting of the passion and veneration of the cross on Good Friday, the singing of *Tenebrae* and the *Exultet* on Holy Saturday, and the celebrations of the Easter fire and the lighting of candles at the Easter Vigil.

As interesting as these developments were, it was often this very elaborate exaltation of liturgy that made some Christians call for reform at the close of the Middle Ages. Protestants critiqued the Catholic theology of transubstantiation, which is what Catholics believe happens during the consecration when the bread and wine truly, completely, and permanently become Jesus' actual Body and Blood in the Eucharist. The Real Presence of Jesus remains in the Eucharist. It does not go away when the congregation disperses, which is why the Eucharist is reserved in a tabernacle. Some Protestants believed in consubstantiation, whereby bread and wine exist along with Jesus' Body and Blood. Others thought that the event at the altar was only a memorial, not a sacrifice, and the bread and wine never ceased being anything but bread and wine. Jesus, in essence, was present in spirit or memory only. Others said that Jesus existed in the community gathered around the altar to remember his death and resurrection.

While Catholics rejected this critique and alternate eucharistic theologies, it remains true that medieval Catholic leaders may not have done such a good job of educating people about the Eucharist and Mass. Faced with the Protestant challenges in this and many other areas of theology and Church organization, the popes and bishops of the Reformation era explicitly emphasized just what the Church does and does not teach about the Eucharist and how she should or should not celebrate Mass. The popes and bishops knew that, during the Middle Ages, the understanding and celebration of the Mass had flagged. The central place where this reeducation effort occurred was the Council of Trent.

Trent affirmed transubstantiation, a word that we saw in chapter three had first been used officially at Lateran IV in 1215 as part of the stipulation that Christians must confess their sins and receive Communion once each year. Trent taught the Real and lasting Presence of Jesus in the Eucharist beyond the consecration and the setting of the Mass. But to make sure that the Mass was celebrated properly both liturgically and theologically, after Trent the popes appointed a liturgical commission to produce books that would guide the liturgies throughout Catholicism. In the fifty years after Trent, this was one of Rome's major efforts.

The first liturgical book published was a Roman breviary in 1568, which guided a priest's daily prayers. In 1570, a *Roman Missal* became the official *Sacramentary*. This *Roman Missal*, mindful of elaborate medieval Masses as well as the cold, dry or private Masses, guided the celebrant in a simplified and clear Mass with some excesses removed. In 1588, a Congregation of Rites was formed in Rome to deal with questions arising about the liturgy, especially those coming from the mission territories in the Americas that had been opened up since Columbus crossed the Atlantic in 1492, which led not only to exploration, but also to evangelization, as well. In 1596, a *Roman Pontifical* was published that guided bishops in their ceremonies and liturgies; in 1614, a *Roman Ritual* followed for the parish priest.

These collections led to a centralized and uniform Mass while clarifying what the Eucharist and Mass mean theologically and sacramentally for Catholics in the context of the many questions raised by the Protestants and the diverse ways they celebrated their liturgies. At the same time that the 1570 *Roman Missal* was made mandatory, it still allowed for a certain diversity in rites that were more than two hundred years old, such as the Ambrosian rite in Milan and the Mozarabic rite in parts of Spain, as long as the diversity did not change the theology of the Eucharist and priesthood. These Catholic Reformations did not remove the private Masses, which left the problem of the overlooked communal aspect of the

Mass unresolved in most places. People still watched rather than participated actively in the Mass. Few received Communion, it is true, but it was certainly hard now to misunderstand that the Eucharist was truly Jesus.

The Mass remained in Latin, although there were several discussions at Trent concerning the use of vernacular languages, which was a thorny issue since the Protestants had quickly moved their liturgies into the dialects of the congregations. Some bishops and theologians at Trent suggested that Mass could be in the vernacular, but certainly that the sermon should be in the people's language. In the end, Trent did not agree with the Protestant idea that the entire liturgy must be in the vernacular. Bishops at the council emphasized that Latin provided a universal language that could unite all Catholics (even though few in the pews knew Latin) and provide a standard and fixed theological vocabulary. Vernacular languages might slip into heresy, they argued, because words in different languages held nuances, and these nuances might lead to different people thinking they believed the same thing when they didn't. But Trent did direct bishops and priests to use vernacular language and not Latin when explaining the sacraments and instructing the congregation in how they should live according to God's commandments. The council also ordered bishops to have the council's teachings on the sacraments translated into the vernacular. Trent may not have gone far enough for some, but many questions about the Mass had been cleared up.

From rubrics to full participation

For several centuries after Trent, we can make a pair of observations about the eucharistic liturgy that seem to comprise a contradiction.

On the one hand, following the rules of liturgy so closely that there was little diversity leads some to see this period as one of rubricism, where priests and bishops followed the rules written in red in the *Sacramentaries* so closely and precisely that Mass felt like a reading of the letter of the law. But at the same time, this was also a period of triumphalism with extravagant art, architecture, and music adorning the liturgy and the Church buildings. We should look at each development in turn.

Rubricism developed, in part, in reaction to the variety of Protestant beliefs and rites that challenged Catholicism and the Mass. While Protestants focused on the priesthood of all believers, it was important to the bishops at Trent to emphasize the ordained priesthood, the Church's authority, and the uniformity of the liturgy. One result was that the priest at the altar became the focal point of the Mass, which distanced the people and discouraged their active participation. The system of private Masses continued as well. In Barcelona alone, requests for private Masses increased eightfold in the sixteenth and seventeenth centuries. Mass remained in Latin and, after 1661, translating *The Roman Missal* into vernacular languages of the people was prohibited. Indeed, approved vernacular missals did not appear in Europe until 1897 and not in the United States until 1927.

Mass did not fall out of favor, however. Church authorities after Trent tried to focus the faithful toward the parish Mass and away from some of the medieval festivals that tended toward superstition. Because more people were attending Mass, parishes often held two and not just one Mass on Sundays. There was also during these early modern centuries an increase in those receiving holy Communion, with some Catholics confessing their sins and receiving the Eucharist four times a year or even monthly, though very rarely drinking from the chalice. The Eucharist remained the high point of the Mass and one that the faithful were directed to worship. Bells rang three times to call their attention to the altar: at the offertory, the elevation, and when the priest received holy Communion.

If rubricism is one end of the story of the early modern Mass, then triumphalism is the other. While parish Masses were more frequent but could be kind of sterile because of liturgical rubricism with very little congregational participation, the physical setting of Masses in major churches across Europe could be quite ornate. The word we usually associate with this triumphalism—referring in the least charitable sense to Catholicism's triumph over Protestantism—is the baroque style of art, architecture, and music that is often described with words like massive, colossal, awe-inspiring, dramatic, and full of the play of light with shadow. The baroque style contrasted sharply with Protestant churches, which were typically very plain, spare, and austere. In addition, the altar had taken a less central spot in Protestant churches since some denominations celebrated a Lord's Supper only once a month. The pulpit to preach the Word of God was made more central and in Calvinist churches often stood right in the center of a round building. Starting in Rome, Catholic baroque architects placed the altar in the central position, raised it up, and lit it with a large dome overhead. In fact, when early modern Catholics entered one of these churches, their eyes were drawn not to the altar but to the tabernacle just above it, which emphasized the Blessed Sacrament.

Other elements of the baroque style emphasized Catholic theology over Protestant ideas. Painters and sculptors portrayed miracles of saints, purgatory, the sacraments, and the life of Mary, the Mother of

God. The Jesuits' church in Rome, the Gesù, was sometimes called a "theater of salvation," and indeed baroque churches are very dramatic. Baroque music created unified musical settings for the entire Mass and not just a few parts. During this period, musicians abandoned secular melodies and instruments for organs and a complex style of music called polyphony that was more ornate than plainsong and most Gregorian chants from the Middle Ages. Baroque music was so operatic that it threatened to overwhelm the Mass and distract from the sacrament the priest was celebrating. After Trent, baroque music yielded to classical and then romantic musical styles, with Masses written by important composers such as Mozart, Haydn, Beethoven and Schubert, each of them making Mass more theatrical. As with many things, well-intentioned people went too far with very good ideas. In the largest basilicas and cities, Mass was becoming a concert or symphony, although the more elaborate the music, the more laypeople were involved as readers and singers, though these tended to be professionals and not the parishioners in the pews. Because Mass was becoming too fancy, in a sense, and more performance than participation, some reformers again raised their voices.

In Italy in the middle of the eighteenth century, for instance, laypeople, priests, and bishops called for increased participation and understanding for the faithful. Some priests followed the letter of the rubrics by reading the Gospel in Latin, but then added a vernacular paraphrase of their own afterward. The most vocal reformers wanted the entire Mass to be translated into the vernacular, but that had to wait more than two centuries until after Vatican II. Other priests did not simply whisper the words of the consecration, but said them loudly and slowly, while some parishes abandoned the simultaneous private Masses at side altars where they still existed in older church buildings. It is clear, then, that during this early modern period, the Mass was being pulled in two directions, leaving to the modern age the task of reconciling the two directions by avoiding their excesses and employing their good sides.

For most Catholics, liturgical change in the modern Church means Vatican II. While it is true that this latest council, which met from 1962–1965, led to massive changes in the Mass, those changes had been developing for over a century. These developments were known as the liturgical movement, which eventually produced the Mass we celebrate today. The key phrase for the liturgical movement is "active participation of the faithful." The enthusiasm for the phrase began largely in France in the nineteenth century, centered on Dom Prosper Guéranger at the Benedictine monastery of Solesmes and spreading to Germany and Belgium. Soon, several academic and popular meetings, journals, and study centers of liturgical practice, designed to help pastors and make parishioners more active in the Mass, appeared in both Europe and North America. One person who read Guéranger's work was Cardinal Giuseppe Sarto, the archbishop of Venice who was later elected Pope Pius X (1903–1914).

As pope, Pius X was particularly interested in enlivening the liturgy and increasing the role and understanding of the person in the pew. With his document *Tra le sollecitudini* in 1903, Pius X encouraged the rediscovery of Gregorian chant, congregational singing, and the active participation of the faithful, including frequent and even daily reception of holy Communion. In 1905, Pius X said that a Catholic who wanted to receive Communion could not be in mortal sin and had to desire to do God's will, but Communion did not have to be the first thing a person ate or drank nor did the Catholic have to go to confession immediately before receiving. In 1910, he dropped the age for first Communion to the age of reason or understanding of the sacrament, which in practice usually became about seven years old. These changes caused both adults and children to learn more about the Mass and the Church's teaching on the Eucharist.

In the 1920s and 1930s in Europe, dialogue Masses grew more popular and increased lay participation. The congregation joined the priest celebrating Mass in saying the Gloria, *Credo, Sanctus,* and *Agnus Dei,* as well as responding to phrases such as *Dominus vobiscum,* all of which remained in Latin, at least officially. More and more, Catholics were not just attending Mass, but celebrating the liturgy with the priest who was presiding. Scholars were writing histories of the Mass and sacred music; laypeople were gathering to discuss the liturgy; and publishers produced small, inexpensive, and jargon-free explanations of Catholic rites and beliefs, especially as they concerned the Mass. The liturgical movement was crossing the Atlantic, too. In the United States, starting in 1926, Virgil Michel at Saint John's Abbey in Collegeville, Minnesota, began a journal, set up a publishing house named Liturgical Press, and held annual meetings on the liturgy.

In the years between World War II and Vatican II, liturgical renewal blossomed. In 1947, Pope Pius XII (1939–1958) established a liturgical commission within the Vatican's Congregation of Rites, which would prove to be the first major step in the organized overhaul of how Mass was celebrated. That same year, the papal document *Mediator Dei* continued Pius X's initiatives, especially in placing the Mass at the center of a Catholic's life. Pius XII allowed some vernacular rites and commissioned a new translation of the psalms. He also approved bilingual Masses for Europe, which allowed priests to use Latin and either French or German. In 1951, the Easter Vigil liturgy was moved to its natural place on Saturday night, and four years later the various Holy Week liturgies were restored and revived. Pius XII approved vernacular hymns in 1953. By the late 1950s, Massgoers would hear the epistle and Gospel first read out in Latin, but then in their vernacular languages. By 1958, laymen (but not women) were permitted to read Scripture at Mass in the vernacular.

For many, the experience of Vatican II's changes came when they went to Mass or attended marriages, baptisms, and funerals in the late 1960s and early 1970s. Vatican II and its key document on the liturgy, *Sacrosanctum concilium*, energized the active participation of the faithful and stressed that people in the congregation must know and understand what is happening at the altar. Soon after the council, the sanctuary was rearranged and holy Communion given under both species. It wasn't long before altar rails disappeared, altars were turned so the priest faced the people, and congregants could receive holy Communion in their hands as the earliest Christians had done. The changes flowed quickly. In 1964, pastors were reminded that they must preach every Sunday and on holy days of obligation. Later that year, the vernacular was approved for the opening greeting, readings, hymns, prayers of the faithful, and the Our Father. In 1967, the *missal, Lectionary*, and eucharistic prayers were revised. In 1971, the vernacular Mass was finally approved, although it had been celebrated for several years already.

Since Vatican II, of course, the liturgy has sometimes been a divisive issue. Those who loved the majesty and mystery of the "old" Mass and others who quickly embraced and ran with every innovation simply because it was new often had unkind words for each other. Some people point out that Vatican II did not specify vernacular liturgies and in fact had said Latin should be preserved, although the Church left it up to local bishops to decide if vernacular was the better way to go. Each side of the debate can point to fringe elements: Mass with soda and cookies on the one hand or the Tridentine Mass celebrated in its full glory on the other. Some Catholics like liturgical dance and altar girls, while others can't stand the ideas. Mass continues to evolve in its forms, although the essentials can never be compromised. Where this will lead is, as always, up to the Holy Spirit, but it is worth remembering that a major source of Catholic unity should and must be the celebration of the Eucharist at Mass.

Discussion questions

- Did anything surprise, disturb, or delight you about the development of the Mass?

- What would you have thought of how Mass was celebrated in the Middle Ages, if you could transport yourself back in time?

- Do you think today's Mass takes the best and avoids the worst of the Church's liturgical history?

- Why do you think Catholics argue so much about how Mass is celebrated?

- There is a saying, "The Eucharist makes the Church." What do you think this saying means?

CHAPTER 5

Sacraments

GRACE FOR THE CATHOLIC JOURNEY

BEFORE WE BEGIN our exploration of how the Church got her seven sacraments, it's important to remember that the idea of development applies especially in this lesson of Church history. For about a thousand years, ideas about the sacraments had some flexibility, which came to be more standardized and fixed under the hands of the scholastic theologians of the Middle Ages. Certain sacraments got more or less attention and discussion in particular periods than others: baptism in the early Church, marriage in the Middle Ages, and orders—especially the permanent diaconate—after Vatican II. (Most of the discussion of the Eucharist has just been treated in chapter four on the Mass.) It was only over the course of many centuries that the theology and practice of these seven sacraments developed from ancient roots into today's practices.

Initiating Christians

Baptism—that is, how to become a Christian—dominated the sacraments in the Church's first few centuries, which makes sense since the Church herself was being born. The first Church communities put baptism (with hints of penance and confirmation) and Eucharist together as what we call sacraments of initiation. A reminder of these roots and the combination of the sacraments of initiation is seen at today's Easter Vigil when adults are baptized, receive the Eucharist, and can be confirmed by the presiding priest if a bishop is not present.

Much of what we know about early baptisms comes from the *Didache*, an instruction manual for Christian initiation and life that may be one of the earliest Church documents, and the *Apostolic Tradition* of Hippolytus from about 225. The baptisms they describe, with an anointing we might be tempted to identify as a separate sacrament of confirmation, typically came after two or three years of preparation and scrutiny, with the final period occurring naturally during Lent. During this process—as is done in today's Church, but over a shorter period of time—the candidates would study the creed and prayers, then at a certain point be tested so that at their baptisms they could declare their faith and its practices for themselves. Just like today's catechumens, potential Christians could attend the Liturgy of the Word, but not the Eucharist. At the Easter Vigil, dressed in white after their baptisms, they would bring up the offertory gifts and receive the Eucharist for the first time.

Early baptisms would be familiar to us: there was a profession of faith and a renunciation of evil. The sign of the cross was made on the forehead and there would be an exchange of peace and a laying on of hands. The new Christian was usually naked and immersed entirely in water three times—once for each person of the Trinity, with an anointing with oil (on the head, hands, or even feet) during or after the immersions. The immersions also represented Jesus' death and resurrection from the dead. The catechumen had to be immersed by someone else: you couldn't baptize (or "clean") yourself, as in certain Jewish purification rituals, which is another example of the early Christian communities moving away from their Jewish roots. The water was supposed to be cold and running, as in a river or stream, but large baths came to be used for practical purposes. For about two hundred years after Jesus, mostly adults were baptized, but infant baptism began to appear early in the third century, with parents answering the questions about the Faith for their children, as godparents do today. By the 400s, infant baptism with godparents seems to have been fairly common except for adult converts.

Tertullian, a north African theologian writing in Latin in the late second and early third century, identified four effects of baptism we might also link with penance and confirmation: remission of sins, deliverance from death, regeneration, and the bestowal of the Holy Spirit. By the early third century, it appears that Christian theologians believed the bestowal of the Holy Spirit was effected not by the waters of baptism but by the anointing with oil, which we can see as the path to confirmation as a distinct sacrament over time.

We find the word "confirmation" used separately in Gaul (modern France) starting in the fifth century. Bishops frequently traveled throughout their dioceses, something like circuit court judges in the nineteenth-century United States. When they visited a particular region, the bishops would confirm all those new Christians who had been baptized since their last visits, regardless of age.

Penance at first occurred just once in a person's lifetime—which is why Christian sympathizers might put baptism off until very late in life—and was a public, communal event that mirrored the catechumenate. The emphasis was originally disciplinary: it was a way of separating the sinner physically from the Church community until he or she could be reconciled back. A model might have been Peter, who denied Christ, felt sorrow and repentance, and then was reconciled with Jesus. Major sins were idolatry, murder, adultery, and incest. John Cassian, a Church Father writing in the early 400s, identified eight others: gluttony, fornication, greed, anger, despair, laziness, vanity, and pride. Penitents could hear the word from the church's lobby and over time work their way up to the front of the congregation, but they couldn't receive the Eucharist, like catechumens. After a period of prayer, penance, good works, and tithing, they were returned to the community during Holy Week, especially Holy Thursday or Good Friday, with the bishop or priest laying hands and offering a prayer of forgiveness.

Penance enjoyed some lively discussions in early medieval Ireland and Wales, where monks played a large role in lay spirituality. Penance moved away from its public, communal, and unrepeatable roots to become private, individual, and repeatable. This development grew partly from a tradition of spiritual direction, where Christians would visit a monk for advice, which mirrored the way monks and nuns sought direction from their abbots and abbesses. Irish missionary monks took this practice with them when they traveled to Gaul, Spain, England, and Italy to evangelize the non-Christians in those regions. What developed was a kind of handbook system, with sins written in one column on a page and the corresponding penance on another. Some of these sound remarkably modern and logically counsel a person to do the opposite of the sin. If a sinner is angry, he should be patient; if he is greedy, he should give freely; if he is gluttonous, he should fast. Often, the penitent was sent away to perform the penance and had to return for absolution. The effort was toward helping penitents change their ways, usually during Lent, through private confession of their sins and a very specific, even practical penance that had to be accomplished before the penitents received absolution. Though private, this notion of penance clearly had a communal dimension: the sinner had to make amends to the person he'd hurt.

We find other sacraments developing in the first millennium of Christianity, too. Anointing of the sick was connected to healing, as it had been for Jesus and the apostles. There is some evidence that the physically or spiritually sick could anoint themselves or even drink blessed oil. Orders or ordinations denoted a certain class or group of people with particular duties. In his *Apostolic Tradition*, Hippolytus tells us that to be a bishop, priest, or deacon there needed to be an ordination, which was comprised of the laying on of hands to call down the Holy Spirit, at least, and often an anointing, too. The community's leaders then appointed readers, acolytes, and other ministers, but these received a prayer and blessing, not the laying on of hands. Certain days came to be customary for ordinations: bishops on Sundays, for example, and priests and deacons on

Saturday evenings. The order of deacons was particularly integral to the early Church. Deacons were married ministers who led prayers and helped at the altar, baptized, and preached. They were closely connected with their bishops and played a special role in teaching catechumens and in helping widows, orphans, and the poor. By the end of the first period of Church history, however, their functions were already being greatly restricted and their golden age was over to await the renewal of the permanent diaconate with Vatican II.

Meanwhile, ordinations became more specific and elaborate as the Middle Ages moved along. A priest being ordained a bishop received a pallium (a circle of cloth around the neck to symbolize his jurisdiction), a Gospel book was placed over his head to show the Church's protection, and he sat on an episcopal throne to show his teaching authority. He was also anointed and invested with a crozier, a miter, and a ring. A new priest received a chalice, bread, and wine; the new deacon was presented with the Gospels. By this time, deacons were almost exclusively transitional in preparation for priesthood. A system of minor orders developed to go with the major ones of bishop, priest, and deacon. These minor orders did not entail ordination but were conveyed with the tool of the order's task: porter (key), lector (*Lectionary*), exorcist (rite for exorcisms), acolyte (candle and cruet), and subdeacon (chalice, paten, cruets, basin, and towel—not unlike today's altar servers).

Marriage in the early Church usually followed society's norms: there need not be a priest or blessing, but there had to be mutual and free consent given by bride and groom with witnesses present. One of the fathers typically presided at home and oversaw the dowry, ring exchange, and the Roman custom of clasping right hands. However, Christians could not divorce, remarry, or marry non-

Christians. As time passed, a blessing by a priest (as opposed to the bride's father) was preferred to make the point that it was God who united the couple. The blessing could take place at the door of the church or in the couple's house—or bedroom—at the time of the engagement or wedding.

Seven sacraments

The rise of scholastic theology in the Middle Ages helped the Church organize and codify her sacraments. The theology professor Peter Lombard (ca. 1100–1160) in Paris synthesized centuries of speculation, debate, and practice concerning sacramental theology to fix the number of sacraments at seven and to explain how they worked. As we've seen, Lateran IV in 1215, building on centuries of speculation and teaching about the Eucharist, used the scholastic word "transubstantiation" to describe how the bread and wine at Mass became the Real Presence of the Body and Blood of Jesus Christ, though it appears to human eyes that bread and wine remain. Lateran IV said Christians should confess their sins and receive the Eucharist once a year, which ended up being referred to as the Easter duty. The age of discretion at which Christians received their first Communion was typically seven to twelve years old.

The individuality of penance continued to develop from the first millennium, although public demonstrations of penance were common in the Middle Ages, especially during Holy Week processions in which penitents (hooded for anonymity) would march through town beating or flailing themselves for their sins. Continuing an earlier procedure, handbooks for private confessions sometimes took a question-and-answer format that the priest could use to guide the penitent through an examination of conscience. Once the sins were identified, the corresponding penance could be assigned. As before, the penitent then left, performed the penitential action, and returned for absolution from the confessor. A formula began to develop for the entire process and we find the Latin phrase *Ego te absolvo...* ("I absolve you...") in common usage by the thirteenth century.

Anointing of the sick became clearer and more formalized, too. During the Middle Ages, the anointing of the sick was restricted to priests: Christians could no longer anoint themselves, which after many centuries finally caught up with the logical parallel that catechumens could not baptize themselves. The anointing was to take place in the context of Mass or at least a prayer service, often connected with the Eucharist and/or penance. There was a laying on of hands and then oil was applied, sometimes with a brush, to the face or head, hands, ears, eyes, mouth, nostrils, and chest. A book of the Scriptures was often held over the sick person's head, as well, with a passage read from James 5:13–16, which speaks of how the earliest Christians prayed with each other, were prayed over and anointed by their elders, confessed their sins, and were forgiven.

Marriage continued its steady march toward becoming a sacrament as we think of it today. The wedding was moved to the church, albeit still only the door and not the altar, at least for commoners; aristocrats and royalty were permitted to stand before the altar. Because there was a frequent concern that the woman was being forced into marriage instead of giving her consent freely, the wedding had to be public and could not be private—secret or clandestine, as it is sometimes called in the sources. The ceremony consisted of the mutual exchange of consent by bride and groom, an instruction by the priest, the bestowal of dowry and ring, and a blessing that, like the rest of the ceremony, was in Latin except for the consent and instruction. All of these rituals still largely mirrored the civil practices for legal reasons, but now were imbued with religious significance and, indeed, sacramentality without a doubt. Church councils paid special attention to the sacrament of marriage. Lateran I (1123) and Lateran II (1139) said that when members of the same family married, they were guilty of incest in the eyes of both Church and civil law. Since medieval Europe was not a very mobile society, this led to problems. Most of the population lived in the countryside where just a few extended families comprised isolated villages separated by fair distances. Christians had to be permitted to marry within a reasonable degree of blood relation, known as consanguinity, or they could not marry and have families at all, practically speaking. How close was too close? Lateran IV in 1215 cleared the matter up: four degrees of separation must be maintained, which in effect meant that a Christian could not marry anyone closer than a second cousin. More than any other sacrament during the Middle Ages, marriage had come into its own.

In retrospect, it was a very good thing indeed that the medieval Church had consolidated her thinking on the sacraments, codified that there were seven, and got a handle on what precisely the sacraments meant and did because during the Reformation period, a variety of Protestant reformers challenged the number and meaning of Catholic sacraments from several angles. The criticisms and challenges concerning Catholicism made in the sixteenth century by Martin Luther, John Calvin, and other Protestant reformers who branched away from them struck at the very heart of the sacramental system because these critiques wondered about essential issues: sinfulness, redemption, and how to get to heaven. Part of

Luther's criticisms were very reasonable and had to do with human excesses—like people snatching up indulgences to pay for the time they would otherwise have to spend in purgatory or to gain the good done by certain penances without actually doing them. But Luther and others went beyond the criticism of the abuse of the indulgence system to say that the very system itself, tied up as it was with the idea that Christians can participate via good works in their salvation, was flawed.

Luther, and Calvin even more so, accentuated God's role in salvation and humanity's sinfulness. While Luther believed that Catholics overemphasized the human dimension and the idea that human actions have merit toward salvation, Calvin knocked humans entirely out of the equation. It was Calvin's position that God and God alone predestined human beings for heaven or hell and nothing that an individual person did could change that fate. This notion attacked the Catholic sacramental system at its core because sacraments are agents of grace that help Catholics improve themselves, turn away from sin, grow closer to God, and work with Jesus to attain eternal salvation. If, as Luther and Calvin said, humans are justified by faith alone, then what role do the sacraments play? And if there is no need for sacraments, what does that mean about the need for priests and their role as mediators, especially given the Protestant principle of the priesthood of all believers?

Luther reduced the number of sacraments to three: baptism, penance, and the Eucharist. He asserted that, while Jesus is really present in the Eucharist, what happened was properly called consubstantiation: the bread and wine remain along with Jesus' Body and Blood. Calvin and his followers kept baptism and the Eucharist, but said Jesus was only symbolically present in bread and wine that never changed at all. For most Protestants, the Mass was not the Catholic sacrifice but only a memorial, which they increasingly called the Lord's Supper. Other Protestants asserted that humans were not born with original sin that had to be wiped clean by baptism, but that Adam and Eve in sinning had only offered a bad example that did not stain human beings after them forever. Baptism therefore was a person's symbolic acceptance of Jesus as his or her Savior or an initiation into the community of believers and so should be undertaken only by adults making a conscious choice, not by infants with godparents speaking for them.

How did Catholicism respond? Among its many explanations, the Council of Trent in the middle of the sixteenth century built on medieval theology to affirm that there were indeed seven sacraments and to describe their natures and purposes. Because Luther and the others had challenged core principles, the council clarified Church teaching on original sin and justification, then explained how the seven sacraments fit within that theology. Trent reached back to Lateran IV (1215) to explain transubstantiation again and to assert that the Eucharist was a sacrament and the Real Presence of Jesus. It also explained what baptism, confirmation, penance, anointing, orders, and marriage were and why they were sacraments, often to counter Protestant ideas. Infant baptism remained, and the role of the godparent was emphasized. The catechism that came out in 1566 to broadcast Trent's teachings in the aftermath of the Protestant Reformations and the Catholic responses supposed that Christians who had been baptized as infants would be confirmed between the ages of seven and twelve when the bishop was available. Christians still received the Eucharist infrequently, but sometimes more than just the Easter duty. Catholics may have received Communion four times a year, which translates into once each season, and some may have received once a month.

Penance also received a boost, with a return to its first millennium roots in private spiritual direction. Manuals something like their early medieval ancestors began to appear after Trent to guide both confessor and penitent, with an emphasis on the continued spiritual growth of the penitent rather than on penance as a quick opportunity to review and dispense with a laundry list of sins. In addition, starting with the years after Trent we begin to see the more common appearance of the confessional box for penance. It was generally set off for privacy but was open: the priest and penitent could be seen, so there could be no opportunity for impropriety. The Church continued to recall penance's roots in private, individual spiritual direction where it was assumed the confessor knew the penitent and could guide him or her appropriately according to the person's unique disposition and spiritual journey. Early in the seventeenth century, a grill came to be installed so the priest and penitent could not see each other, which gave anonymity to the penitent and was in fact somewhat new. Penance had long lost its public dimensions and had now become not only private, but anonymous.

As we move into the early modern period, Mass remained the focus of parish life and was celebrated with vigor in Europe's large cities down to her small villages. But Catholicism in Britain's American colonies was a minority religion in an Anglican setting. Although Catholicism was not outlawed in the sense Christianity had been during the first few centuries of her life in the Roman Empire, Roman Catholic practice was relegated to second-class status and had to deal with some harsh attitudes. In 1704, the Anglican British governor of the Maryland colony referred to Catholic Masses as gaudy shows.

Catholics largely celebrated Mass in small groups in private chapels in homes or simply in a house's dining or living room. Some Colonial American Catholics received Communion as much as once a month, but most probably received three to four times per year. Mass was not always available every Sunday at a convenient location since there were few priests, especially before the American Revolution. Early in the nineteenth century, penance was celebrated by most people about once a year, with once a month for those few Catholics who were especially fervent and had access to a priest with some regularity. Communion and penance were therefore more common in the few cities than in the many small villages, a circumstance that was true around the globe.

Anointing of the sick had, over the course of the Middle Ages and Reformations, come to be offered most commonly on a person's deathbed, which gave it the popular names extreme unction (typically garbled as something sounding like "extramunction") or last rites. This remained true as the centuries advanced toward modernity. The rite involved was shortened—understandably, since time was often an issue with a dying person—and came to be known as *viaticum*. The rite included the reception of Communion and confession with absolution, if that were possible given the physical state of the dying person.

Marriage during this early modern period sometimes became, at least for elites, more legalistic and supervised since inheritance issues were involved. In Colonial America and after the American Revolution, mixed marriages between Catholics and non-Catholics were uncommon but they did occur, perhaps with relatively greater frequency than in Europe, where the memory of the Protestant-Catholic split remained and was more relevant socially and politically.

The marriage rite itself was now definitively moved to the altar, where the exchange of consent was always witnessed by a priest with the family taking a secondary role. Local customs were permitted: it was still common for a priest to bless the marriage bed.

The sacraments of initiation were continuing to solidify around certain ages. Infant baptism, except for adult converts, had been the norm for many centuries. Confirmation was still celebrated almost exclusively when the bishop came to certain locations on the regular visits to every region of his diocese that Trent had made mandatory for diocesan bishops. While that meant no individual age was the one set up as preferable for confirmation, in practice young Catholics were confirmed between the ages of seven and twelve, which agreed with Trent's catechism. First Communion, contrary to current practice, often came after confirmation and not before. The common age for first Communion was eleven or twelve. Even during these early modern centuries, some theologians, bishops, and pastors thought first Communion should come before confirmation, which demonstrates that sacramental theology continued to develop on the eve of modernity.

Practice and renewal

Vatican II's late-twentieth-century changes are perhaps nowhere more visible than in the way we celebrate the sacraments. We should stress, though, that certain movements to increase the celebration and understanding of the sacraments predated Vatican II in the 1960s and paved the way for more developments—many with roots deep in ancient Church practices—in the council's aftermath. The three sacraments that have most noticeably evolved since the council have been penance, anointing of the sick, and within orders the renewal of the permanent diaconate.

Some readers may still recall Saturday's long lines to the confessional that predated the council, often as a way of lamenting that no one goes to confession any more. One study showed, for example, that in 1963, thirty-seven percent of American Catholics surveyed went to confession once a month, but by 1974 that figure had fallen to seventeen percent. Those long lines date back to the middle of the nineteenth century, when parish missions grew in popularity. Under the guidance of Redemptorist and Paulist preachers especially, missions focused on a return to the sacraments, especially to Communion via penance. In 1974, the rite was altered to emphasize dialogue and instruction. The very language of the sacrament changed from confession and penance to reconciliation. Confessional boxes were reconfigured into reconciliation rooms that gave the penitent the option of celebrating the sacrament face-to-face or in anonymity. The rite includes an examination of conscience beforehand, which is sometimes part of a communal service, then private confession of sins, instruction, an assignment of penance—which, as with its origins, can be tied into making amends with a person offended, including God—a statement of contrition, and absolution at that time. This renewal has drawn more laypeople into the regular practice of spiritual direction, which reaches all the way back into Church history.

Anointing of the sick has moved away from extreme unction, although Catholics and non-Catholics alike still incorrectly refer to the last rites, especially in dramatic news reports about a Catholic's death. The emphasis is now on a sacrament that can be repeated, need not be administered at the point of death (or even danger of death), and that helps people of various ages who are sick physically and emotionally. Anointing of the sick, with its renewed emphasis on healing, has become a gift to those facing operations and chronic illnesses.

The most important modern development in orders was the renewal of the diaconate, with permanent deacons who can be married. The movement began in nineteenth-century Germany and took hold especially in Europe and Africa after World War II. Pope Paul VI approved the permanent diaconate's restoration in 1967, and the next year the first permanent deacons were ordained in Germany and Cameroon. Americans followed in 1969, with nearly half of the world's permanent deacons now serving in the United States.

Marriage now enjoys a greater understanding among brides and grooms that they, and not the witnessing priest, celebrate the sacrament by marrying each other. Couples participate more in the marriage ceremony by selecting their readings, but the rite itself retains much from earlier Church history: a welcome, the free giving of consent, holding right hands, an exchange of vows and rings (with the man now often wearing one, too), the nuptial blessing, and local customs. Vatican II also emphasized the family's sacred role as the domestic Church built on the sacrament of marriage.

In 1969, the rites for marriage, infant baptism, and funerals were updated; the same year, Paul VI issued a new General Instruction for celebrating the sacraments. The confirmation rite was revised and the Rite of Christian Initiation of Adults (RCIA) was restored in the early 1970s. RCIA especially returned the Church to the initiation roots of her first few centuries. Unfortunately, confirmation is in danger of losing its significance as one of the sacraments of initiation and—in its worst-case scenario—can be the sacrament of exit because young people may never return to church afterward, unless it is to be married. Some liturgists believe confirmation should be held back until adulthood, when mature people can really say for themselves that they want to accept the responsibility of being an adult Catholic—something akin to Protestant evangelicals who are typically born again as college students or later—but others fear that this would mean fewer confirmations. This discussion is another reminder that, while the Church cherishes her seven sacraments, how precisely they are celebrated is a matter that will likely continue to develop.

Discussion questions

- In your experience, does the Church combine old and new in her celebration of the sacraments?

- Where—and how—do you think the Church could do a better job in explaining her sacraments?

- What sacraments do you think need attention now? How might you invigorate them?

- Explore how you experience the sacraments as they relate to the life, death, and resurrection of Jesus, and to the process of salvation.

- Of the seven sacraments, which one affects you most personally? Why?

CHAPTER 6

Other Faiths

HOW CATHOLICS WALK WITH NON-CATHOLICS

First outsiders, then insiders

When Christianity came on the scene in the Roman Empire, it was considered a strange and confusing movement. Some Jews wondered whether Christianity was a branch of their faith or something new entirely. Romans considered Christians pagans because they didn't follow the established polytheism of many Greco-Roman gods and goddesses that was closely tied to the Roman political and social systems. To be a Jew or a Christian was to be an enemy of the state, a traitor, an outsider, and an atheist. So Christianity's first task was to establish its own identity: not Jewish, not pagan and polytheistic, and certainly not dangerous.

A group of Christians set out to explain Christianity to non-Christians: the apologists. They did not apologize as we understand the term today—no one should have to say he is sorry to be a Christian or a follower of any religion—but the word "apologist" describes a person who explains. They used emerging creeds, liturgical celebrations, and the writings called gospels and letters to explain what Christians believed and why they acted the way they did. Fundamentally, Romans valued this world, while Christians looked to the next, which put Christians out of step with the dominant society in which they lived. Apologists had to dance delicately: to explain what Christians believed, but also to convince Romans why Christians should not be considered subversive because of those beliefs.

Apologists tended to be aristocratic Roman citizens who, once converted to Christianity, used their training in Greco-Roman philosophy to explain Christianity in ways that the pagan Romans could understand. They tried to persuade the pagans that Christians were good citizens and not members of a socially undermining cult or rebels who were mysterious and couldn't be trusted. Rather, they emphasized that the Christian message was open to all. To do so, they took different approaches in explaining Christianity to Roman and Greek pagans. Justin Martyr, for instance, was a pagan convert to Christianity who didn't go through a Jewish stage in his development. Born in Palestine about 100 into a wealthy pagan Greek family, he found Greek philosophy failed to satisfy him. After his conversion, he traveled to Rome, established a school of apologetics there, and wrote several tracts that had a distinctly dispassionate tone. One of his major points was philosophical: the soul could not attain direct communion with God without the Holy Spirit. But Justin was not a cold academic: in 165, he was beheaded for the Faith.

Another apologist document, the anonymous Letter to Diognetus from about the year 150, has a more approachable and catechetical style. The author explained that while pagans worshipped God's creations, such as idols made of wood or stone, Christians worshipped God. This letter stressed Christianity's fundamental monotheism, which would have been out of step with Roman polytheism, but it also pointed out that Christians and Romans had common ground in ethical values like the virtues, stability, and peace on which the *Pax Romana* was built. Another apologist, Athenagoras, wrote a letter explaining Christianity to the Roman emperor about 175–180. He countered the popular charges against Christians: that they engaged in incest, cannibalism, and were untrustworthy atheists because they did not believe in the Roman gods. Christianity, he said, was in harmony and not in competition with Greco-Roman philosophy, social values, and political stability.

Because Romans had some experience with Jews, the apologists sometimes started with the Old Testament to show how the prophets foretold of the Jesus of the New Testament as well as to demonstrate that the God of the Old Testament was the Father of the New Testament's Jesus. Christian authority came from Scripture and the apostles, which made Christianity less frightening as something entirely new with no past. There is a negative side, however, and this came when Christian apologists tried too hard to distinguish Christianity from Judaism and ended up denigrating Jews. What we find is a pair of strands of Christian attitudes toward the Jews in the early Church. Both strands can be found in Paul. In the Letter to the Romans, Paul implies that the kingdom of God is spiritual (Christian) and not made up of flesh (Jewish). But in Galatians and 1 Corinthians, Jews are identified with Ishmael, Abraham's son with Hagar, and so should be expelled as they'd been. The Letter to Diognetus refers to the Jews as wrong, foolish, and superstitious. Augustine (354–430) noted that Jews give witness to the Old Testament prophecies of Christ, although he identified them with Cain, who had killed Abel. John Chrysostom (ca. 347–407) referred to Jews as degenerates and dogs, adding that any Christian fraternizing with Jews or failing to block such fellowship is God's enemy.

As Christianity moved out of her first stage of development in the early Church, two features should be noted. First, the two strands of attitudes toward Jews would continue to develop, though the negative strand grew fiercer. Second, Christianity had moved from being a persecuted to a favored religion in the fourth century, and so her efforts at spreading the Faith came no longer from an inferior position, but from the most central place in society. This change in status would influence how Christians related to other faiths in the rest of the first millennium, where the primary question concerned evangelization and inculturation. How could Christianity best spread the Gospel message to heretics, such as Arians who held that Jesus was not fully God, and to European pagans?

The practical strategy came down to this: missionaries assimilated pagan rituals, sites, and holy people without giving up too much of Christianity. Otherwise, what resulted would not be new Christians but, at best, Christianized pagans. This strategy came largely from Pope Gregory the Great (590–604), who was intensely interested in spreading the Faith. In an influential letter that he sent to a French abbot named Mellitus, who was on his way to England in 601, the pope advised a soft and pragmatic approach:

Gregory said, "...[T]he temples of idols in that nation should not be destroyed, but...the idols themselves that are in them should be. Let blessed water be prepared and sprinkled in these temples and altars constructed and relics deposited since, if these same temples are well built, it is needful that they should be transferred from the worship of idols to the service of the true God; that, when the people themselves see that these temples are not destroyed, they may put away error from their heart and, knowing and adoring the true God, may have recourse with the more familiarity to the places they have been accustomed to....Nor let them any longer sacrifice animals to the devil, but slay animals to the praise of God for their own eating, and return thanks to the Giver of all....For it is undoubtedly impossible to cut away everything at once from hard hearts, since one who strives to ascend to the highest place must needs rise by steps or paces, and not by leaps."

How did this strategy play out? Missionaries found in the pagans a predisposition to faith in the supernatural that made their jobs easier: these people were not atheists, but religious believers already, although they did not believe in Jesus. They tried to channel the pagans' innate religious enthusiasm and their sense of wonder, awe, fear, and respect toward Christianity. Some of the most interesting places where this happened were Visigothic Spain, Merovingian and Carolingian Gaul (France), and Anglo-Saxon England in the seventh through the ninth centuries.

Missionaries did not replace the pagans' religious objects and actions, but assigned a greater source or person to them. While pagans might pay more attention to an action such as a physical cure or to the person performing the action (a *magus* or *medicus*), missionaries called these cures miracles and assigned them to God acting through saints, who were not curing for the money as were pagan ministers. Restoring health, therefore, remained a special mark—not of magic but of holiness. This might strike us as superstitious, but in the first millennium the Church permitted the idea that bells blessed by a holy person (a priest, bishop, abbot, or hermit) could dispel fever or thunder if rung in the right circumstances. It was also common to believe that dust from a saint's tomb, when sprinkled on the eyes of a blind person, could restore sight. The Church condemned prophecy or soothsaying by reading an animal's entrails, the flight of birds, or the path of the stars, but missionaries allowed people to believe in angels and demons, the power of relics, and the idea that God could speak to believers in dreams.

Christians could not worship nature and astrology, but they could learn from the moon's waxing and waning the moral lesson that, in any life, there are good times and bad. Wood was not holy in itself, but the wood of the cross was an instrument of salvation. Fountains were not sacred, but it was smart to build baptismals at the site of sacred springs, which allowed old pagan allegiances to be reassigned to Christian faith, which is just what Pope Gregory had in mind. The most spectacular example would be the alleged amulet of Charlemagne: two crystal hemispheres bound with gold and worn on a chain around the neck, with a bit of the True Cross and a strand of the Blessed Virgin Mary's hair. In this way, the pagan reverence for wood and hair was transferred to a Christian relic.

These centuries also saw Christianity relating to a new faith. Islam came on the scene with Mohammed (ca. 570–632), who shared Allah's revelations in the Koran and spread Islam through present-day Saudi Arabia. After his death, Islam expanded rapidly in just one century. Muslims took control of the Holy Land, moved westward across north Africa, turned up in the Iberian peninsula (today's Spain and Portugal), then crossed the Pyrenees until 732, when Charlemagne's grandfather Charles Martel turned them back at the battle of Tours. The Mediterranean Sea, for centuries called a Roman lake, was now Mohammed's lake. Christianity was cut off from its Greek, eastern borders and roots. How Muslims, Christians, and Jews interacted in the aftermath of this spectacular spread is a story better told from the vantage point of the Middle Ages and the Crusades.

Competition and conflict

Since Islam's appearance and rapid spread in the 600s and early 700s, Christians had lived under Muslim rule quite peaceably, although there were also episodes of violence. Like the Jews, Christians were protected minorities in lands controlled by Islam. Both Christians and Jews paid a tribute tax, but were largely left alone to practice their faith, live their lives, and they were not pressed to convert. While Christian pilgrims to the Holy Land were sometimes harassed, assaulted, and even killed during the Middle Ages, Muslims did not want to stem the tide of pilgrims because of the income to be attained from allowing Christians to visit the Church of the Holy Sepulchre in Jerusalem and the other holy sites in Bethlehem, Nazareth, Bethany, and elsewhere. This status was different than the state of affairs under Christian rule: on the whole, it was harder for Jews and Muslims to live, worship, and work freely in Christian countries.

For those who had a basic understanding of the other's faith, there was some respect and understanding. Jesus and Mary are revered by Muslims, although Islam does not recognize Jesus as the Son of God and the Messiah. Jesus is the greatest prophet, second only to Mohammed, in Islam. Informed Muslims saw Christianity as a revelation of God, but not the full revelation as represented by Islam. Both were people of law and justice; they agreed on God as the creator of the universe; and some Christians and Muslims understood their shared heritage concerning Abraham and one God. But Muslims could not understand how God could be one and three at the same time, which made the concept of the Trinity completely alien to them—so much so that they recorded Crusader oaths taken "in the name of the Father, the Son, and the Holy Spirit" as "by God, by God, by God." Nor could most Muslims understand how God could be born of a woman, live as a child, and die.

The Crusades provided a volatile context for relations among Christians, Jews, and Muslims. By the time of the First Crusade (1095–1099), the cultural groundwork had been laid for large-scale Christian violence against the Jews. Medieval Jews were sometimes accused of cheating Christian businessmen, desecrating the consecrated host, holding "black" masses with the devil, and slaughtering Christian children, especially around Passover, so they could make matzo with the blood, known as the infamous "blood libel." Jews were outsiders in Christian Europe: they could not be guild members, hold land, or be town officials because of the Christian oaths involved. Specifically, there was a dangerous precedent linking Jews, Christians, Muslims and the Holy Land about a century before the first Crusade. In 1009, a caliph named Hakim ordered the destruction by fire of the Church of the Holy Sepulchre. A decade later, a group of French Christians claimed the Jews in their local area had put the Muslim Hakim up to it and even paid him, which led to the forced mass baptism and slaughter of these Jews.

Two sets of major attacks were made on Jews by Christians on their way to fight the Muslims in the Holy Land. The first set of pogroms followed the calling of the first Crusade in 1095, and the second was related to the second Crusade in 1145. As the first Crusaders left, some asked themselves why they were traveling so far to attack the "infidel" Muslims when the "infidel" Jews were right next door. Pogroms occurred in the spring of 1096, very soon after Pope Urban II called for the Crusade in 1095, in Speyer, Mainz, Cologne, other towns along the Moselle valley, Prague, and Ratisbon. The scenes were repeated in the spring of 1146 in connection with the second Crusade, with most of the violence occurring in towns and villages in the Rhineland. The violence was extreme, with some Jews choosing to commit suicide rather than give themselves up to forced conversion or death.

Not all Christians were guilty. A number of bishops sheltered Jews and, although some later decided to withdraw their protection, a few put their own lives on the line, faced the crowds calling for Jewish blood, and saved Jewish lives. The Cistercian abbot Bernard of Clairvaux (1090–1153), who preached the second Crusade on the pope's command, was enraged at the attacks against Jews. He wrote one letter denouncing a monk who claimed to have been sent by God to promote the Crusade and to tell the armies to start with the Jews. In another document, an open letter to the English people, Bernard was blunt: "I have heard with great joy of the zeal for God's glory which burns in your midst, but your zeal needs the timely restraint of knowledge. The Jews are not to be persecuted, killed, or even put to flight." In language that seems like a back-handed endorsement, he said it was better to convert the Jews: "The Jews are for us the living words of Scripture, for they remind us always of what our Lord suffered. They are dispersed all over the world so that by expiating their crime they may be everywhere the living witnesses of our redemption."

As we move into the fifteenth century and beyond, the story of how the Church related to other faiths changes dramatically for two reasons. The first is the fact that the world doubled after Columbus, with new opportunities to spread the Faith to people who were not monotheists and who had no connection to European civilization. The second reason is that the Church's unity shattered into Catholic and Protestant Christians, with Protestantism itself subdivided into a number of denominations: Lutherans, Calvinists, Anglicans, Anabaptists, Methodists, etc.

European monarchs saw it as their royal duty to patronage missionaries. Popes were happy to give kings and queens fairly free rein, since they were paying for and physically protecting the missions. In 1508, Pope Julius II (1503–1513) went so far as to grant Spain's Ferdinand and Isabella ecclesiastical rights: the monarchs paid the clergy, established dioceses, built churches, and named bishops. Encounters, however, were often brutal. The indigenous populations of the Americas were told to become Christians or face slavery or sometimes death. Mass baptisms in the Americas and in India make us wonder how Christian these converts really were, which was a question dating all the way back to Charlemagne's forced conversions in the early Middle Ages. Soon, provincial councils in sixteenth-century Peru warned against quick baptisms, emphasizing catechesis instead. But explorers often simply wiped out whatever native faith was in their way, which happened in Hernando Cortés' 1519–1521 massacre of the Aztecs in modern-day Mexico and Francisco Pizarro's conquest of the Incas in Peru that same century. When Ferdinand Magellan arrived in 1521 in the Philippines, he set up a large cross for Easter Sunday and made all the native leaders venerate it. One village that refused was burned to the ground, causing the battle in which Magellan was himself killed. North American missionaries regularly referred to the indigenous populations around the Great Lakes in modern-day Canada and the United States as savages.

There was also another approach. Other missionaries, perhaps unconsciously building on the first millennium methods of Pope Gregory the Great, learned native languages for their catechesis classes. Baptism, confession, and marriage were freely offered, though holy Communion and sometimes ordinations were withheld. Most famously, the Jesuits realized that to succeed in China and Japan, they had to adapt to the culture by dressing as wise men and accommodating Christianity to Asian ideas instead of imposing Europe's foreign Latin and western culture. The Jesuit Matteo Ricci (1552–1610) entered China dressed as a Buddhist monk, learned Chinese, studied Confucius, dressed as a scholar, and finally converted members of the imperial court to Christianity. Jesuits in Brazil learned the local languages and customs, taught catechesis, and only baptized after sufficient instruction.

In 1568, Pope Pius V instituted the Congregation of Cardinals for the Conversion of Infidels (whose last word certainly places the action in its historical context). In 1622, the papacy established the Congregation for the Propagation of the Faith, which brought together a number of Roman departments and earlier efforts concerned with the missions. What the popes were doing was trying to assert control over the kings who thought they were in charge of Christianity in the new territories, as they had essentially been for about a century. The Roman concern may sound surprisingly forward-thinking: the Church wanted missionaries not to institute a European Christianity and clergy, which was the royal method, but to establish an indigenous Christianity with a local clergy as quickly as possible.

The second major way the Church related to other faiths in this period was the conflict within Europe: Christianity split into Roman Catholics, on the one hand, and a variety of Protestant churches, on the other. After Luther posted his *Ninety-Five Theses* in 1517 and religious, social, and political tumult ensued, the first time things settled down was the Peace of Augsburg in 1555, which allowed rulers to choose either Catholicism or Lutheranism for their territories. A truce lasted until 1618, when the Thirty Years War broke out between German Catholics and Protestants. The fight spread across Europe with countries lining up into a Protestant Union versus a Catholic League, although even within these two umbrellas there was infighting. With the Peace of Westphalia in 1648, Europe was largely split three ways: Catholics, Lutherans, and Calvinists (called Huguenots in France). This treaty stipulated that a ruler could not impose his religion, but he could regulate public worship while permitting private worship.

There are several bottom lines to this part of the story. First, religion itself suffered and became devalued. It was a major influence in people's lives, to be sure, but it was now just one of several major influences along with social change, political upheaval, and cultural unrest. Second, the Protestant criticisms and the Catholic responses ushered in a period not of ecumenism, but of religious conflict and theological debate—a Christian cold war. Catholics and Protestants rarely spoke with each other; instead, they yelled at each other. Diatribe replaced what little dialogue there had been. Polemicists and apologists on both sides of the Christian divide wrote academic treatises and popular essays designed to show why their version of Christianity was right and the others were wrong. Third, and more positively, the missions became a place where Christianity could spread. Catholics at first established missions far more than Protestants did, in large part because Catholicism's central organization facilitated such efforts. Over the centuries, Protestants turned to the missions, too, especially in Africa and Asia during the imperial and colonial periods of the early modern and modern world, where they, too, faced the interesting challenges of balancing inculturation, assimilation, and accommodation when they encountered polytheistic faiths.

Global approaches

In the period after the Council of Trent concluded in 1563, missionaries took different approaches to converting indigenous populations in the Americas, Asia, and Africa. While some missionaries, especially in the Americas, tended to convert from the bottom of society and move upward, in Asia the effort was largely to target the top of society and work downward, which is what had tended to occur in northern Europe in the first millennium. In both cases, the missionaries tried to develop a clergy from the indigenous population as soon as possible, but continued the general movement of preventing them from joining religious orders.

The missions were directed by two separate congregations established in Rome: the Propagation of the Faith in Africa and the Propagation of the Faith in Asia. In 1659, a directive from the office for Asia—reminiscent of Pope Gregory I's instructions to a missionary on his way to England over a thousand years before—indicated a measure of openness to indigenous believers and customs rather than a heavy-handed approach:

"Do not demand of those peoples that they change their ceremonies, customs, and habits if these do not quite obviously contradict religion and decency, for what could be sillier than to want to import France, Spain, Italy, or any other country into China? Not these but the Faith is what you shall bring to them, which neither rejects nor fights against any peoples' customs and traditions, but rather seeks to keep them inviolate."

Meanwhile, in the Americas the Franciscans took a fairly strong, even militaristic approach that sometimes forced Christianity onto people. The Franciscans were not the only religious order who could be heavy-handed: history records that religious orders including the Jesuits held slaves in North, Central, and South America. Others were, in one way or another, connected with the slave trade at its source, in Africa, where their efforts to evangelize were tangled and slowed by tribal warfare, by European slave traders who were penetrating the African continent along with missionaries, and by frequent reversals of fortune.

Some missionaries may have taken a strong, even violent, approach because of the fear or danger of syncretism, whereby Christianity would take on so many indigenous beliefs and practices that the Faith lost her essentials and stopped being authentic Christianity. This concern led the archbishop of Lima in Peru to order idolatry inspections in 1640. A strict hand could be used to ward syncretism off, which led one eighteenth-century Mayan to remark that he hoped Christ would appear in his Second Coming so he would throw out the Spanish and restore the Mayan kingdoms and social structures.

One way to approach this question is by looking at the Jesuit missions in Asia and especially the Chinese Rites Controversy. While it's sometimes hard to pin down precisely what the Chinese Rites were, it appears they included some ceremonies honoring Confucius, ancestor worship, and the adoption of Chinese ideas approximating heaven and an omniscient God that seemed close enough to Christian concepts. Jesuit missionaries in China also tapped into a Chinese philosophy that was predisposed to monotheism and emphasized a concept of ethics rather than a list of sins. They only rarely displayed a crucifix, since the symbol of a dead God (as some put it) puzzled the Chinese. The stage was set, therefore, to slip into syncretism if the Jesuits were not careful and went too far down the road of accommodation. How did Rome respond? The answer is: with mixed signals. In 1603, a Jesuit official allowed ancestor worship and the ceremonies for Confucius. Pope Paul V (1605–1621) approved saying Mass in Chinese. Then, in 1645, Rome condemned ancestor worship, but in 1656, Pope Alexander VII approved the Jesuit strategy. From 1705 to 1715, some European monarchs who were bankrolling the Jesuit missions backed their approach, but about the same time Pope Clement XI reasserted the condemnation of ancestor worship. In 1745, Pope Benedict XIV finally prohibited the Chinese Rites.

Interreligious competition and inculturation questions followed the Church for two centuries until Vatican II (1962–1965) built on decades of very slow and careful steps to dramatically change the way Catholicism related to people of other faiths. So much changed at Vatican II and in its aftermath that we can look at this part of Church history as a prime example of how the Church develops.

In its document on missionary activity, *Ad gentes* (1965), the council noted specifically that the opportunity to expand the Faith in diverse cultures requires a variety of perspectives and approaches as well as a respect for local custom. *Ad gentes* specifically prohibited forced conversions and repeated the Church's long-standing policy of promoting an indigenous clergy. The document on ecumenism, *Unitatis redintegratio* (1964), viewed the past history of Protestants and Catholics with frankness and sadness, but hoped for a better future. It recognized that there was plenty of blame to go around but instructed Catholics to go in a different direction by engaging Protestants in dialogue with a spirit of respect and learning, never forgetting their common bond in Jesus. Since then, great progress— though not without significant stumbles—has taken place as people of many Christian faiths (Orthodox, Anglican, Lutheran, etc.) have tried to move closer together by studying key theological concepts, human institutions, and historical developments.

For our story we should take special care to look back to the medieval heritage among Jews, Muslims, and Christians to see the change brought about by Vatican II. We begin with the Church and Jewish people. In recent years especially, there has been quite a debate about the degree to which the Catholic Church and individual Christians have or have not contributed to a mainstream anti-Semitism that can be found throughout Western history. At the same time, Pope John Paul II particularly tried to improve relations between Jews and Christians, specifically Catholics. On several occasions, he referred with great respect to the Jews as the Christians' elder brothers and sisters. He has also apologized for the violence against the Jews that was a terrible part of Church history. In March 2000, he visited Israel, prayed at Yad Vashem (Israel's Holocaust memorial and museum), and left a note in the Western Wall asking forgiveness for the sins committed by members of the Church against Jews throughout history. Indeed, the idea that all Jews—past, present, and future—were guilty of Jesus' murder was a standard belief changed only officially when Vatican II issued *Nostra aetate* (1965): "True, the Jewish authorities and those who followed their lead pressed for the death of Christ; still, what happened in his passion cannot be charged against all the Jews, without distinction, then alive, nor against the Jews of today. Although the Church is the new people of God, the Jews should not be presented as rejected or accursed by God, as if this followed from the holy Scriptures....[T]he Church, mindful of the patrimony she shares with the Jews and moved not by political reasons but by the Gospel's spiritual love, decries hatred, persecutions, displays of anti-Semitism, directed against Jews at any time and by anyone."

The Church has also sought to improve her official relations with Muslims. Paul VI in *Ecclesiam Suam* (1964) noted: "Then we have those worshipers who adhere to other monotheistic systems of religion, especially the Muslim religion. We do well to admire these people for all that is good and true in their worship of God." The next year at Vatican II, the document *Lumen gentium* stated: "But the plan of salvation also includes those who acknowledge the Creator. In the first place amongst these there are the Mohammedans, who, professing to hold the faith of Abraham, along with us adore the one and merciful God, who on the last day will judge mankind."

Since then, Church leaders around the world have also spoken with respect for other ancient world religions, including Hinduism and Buddhism. In October 1999, an interreligious assembly met in Rome and agreed on several joint statements, including the important recognition that coming and praying together does not mean that any one group must give up its identity to any other. Rather, the assembly called on each faith tradition to work with the others, to learn and to teach, and to find common ground while understanding key differences with greater depth. The leaders did not seek to whitewash the dark chapters in history but to condemn hatred and to seek a shared path of reconciliation for the future.

We should return to Pope John Paul II, since he did so much to improve the relations between Catholics and people of other faiths. In his statement on the third millennium, *Novo Millennio Ineunte* (2001), he said:

"It is in this context [of openness to God's grace] also that we should consider the great challenge of inter-religious dialogue to which we shall still be committed in the new millennium, in fidelity to the teachings of the Second Vatican Council. In the years of preparation for the Great Jubilee the Church has sought to build, not least through a series of highly symbolic meetings, a relationship of openness and dialogue with the followers of other religions. This dialogue must continue. In the climate of increased cultural and religious pluralism which is expected to mark the society of the new millennium, it is obvious that this dialogue will be especially important in establishing a sure basis for peace and warding off the dread spectre of those wars of religion which have so often bloodied human history. The name of the one God must become increasingly what it is: a name of peace and a summons to peace."

The times, indeed, have changed.

Discussion questions

- What did you find surprising and/or upsetting about this aspect of Church history?

- Do you think Catholics should emphasize what they share or how they are different from other Christians?

- Do you think Catholics should emphasize what they share or how they are different from people of other faiths?

- Why do you think a particular expression of Christianity tries to say its version of Christianity is better than others? Why do you think a believer of any religious tradition tries to one-up other religious traditions?

- How might you follow the Church's directions to foster dialogue in your home community?

CHAPTER 7

Laity

LIVING THE FAITH

Separating laity and clergy

The first thing to notice about laypeople from the historical evidence of the early Church is something that's not there. We can't find the word "laity" in the Old Testament or the New Testament—at least a laity as distinct from a clergy. We do find with some frequency the important word *laos*, which at various places in the Bible indicates a people, a nation, Israel, and the new people of God. The word *laos* in the Bible denotes not only ministers, but those they served; there is no clear distinction yet, although the Hebrew people did have a priestly class with specific liturgical functions, specifically in the temple.

The Old Testament contains the idea of a new people of God who believed in one divinity, which separated them from their polytheistic and pagan neighbors in the ancient Mesopotamian and Mediterranean worlds. This new people of God became a new people of Christ in earliest Christianity. By the middle of the first century, we begin to find the word "laity" rarely, though it probably refers to this new people of Christ and not a particular class of laypeople as opposed to a separate group of clergy. But as the second century proceeds, we see a developing division between the *ordo* (order) of people in leadership positions who had been ordained and the *ordo* of people who were not ordained, though some of these acted as ministers of charity, teachers, and apologists just as they do today.

The state of being a layperson or a clergy member was increasingly based on how you lived your Christian life—what actions you performed and how those actions were officially sanctioned by the Church: with ordination or without ordination. In turn, certain actions were associated with the different states of life: priests led liturgies and laypeople participated in them by praying, singing, walking in processions, receiving Communion, seeking penance, and taking part in other devotional and service actions. Each had its particular role.

We find many examples of laypeople living their faith as actively as the ordained ministers. Many laypeople kept the Faith along with their clergy members during the Roman persecutions in the first four centuries of Christianity. They earned the crown of martyrdom with their priests and bishops—and sometimes without them when some priests and bishops denied the Faith to save their lives. In north Africa and the East especially, laypeople were involved in Church affairs as teachers, catechists, and theologians, taking part in the great debates concerning doctrine. The theologian Gregory Nazianus reported that he heard laypeople arguing about Christ's humanity and divinity in the markets of Constantinople in 379. It's clear, then, that the laity were not second-class citizens in the early Church.

After Christianity became tolerated by the Roman Empire and then was established as the only official and legitimate religion in the fourth century, we can see a clearer line between laity and an ordained clergy. Especially as the empire steadily fell apart, priests and bishops became local leaders, offering service not only to the Church, but also to the broader society by negotiating treaties, collecting taxes, overseeing public welfare, and maintaining roads and bridges. The more powerful and wealthier laity also served the Church by working as advisers to clerical leaders as well as to lay rulers. However, there was an unfortunate tendency in this period as the two orders separated to see the laity as a second or lower class of Christians, allegedly because they did not lead lives of poverty, chastity, and obedience. Not every priest or bishop did, either, and both orders had worldly duties that they often carried out faithfully and honorably. Because the perception was that the clerical *ordo* was a higher or even purer way to live the Faith, the idea grew that to be a better Christian, you had to join the clergy. Since the clergy were becoming leaders of society, the path to political power sometimes ran through a Church's aisles and schools, and not just down a strictly lay road.

Laypeople are sometimes seen as passive and even negative toward the clergy—certainly an unfair characterization since recent studies identify a very vibrant spiritual life for laymen and women struggling to keep the Faith during these harsh centuries. We have indications toward the end of the first millennium of laypeople gathering to share particular devotions (such as to a local saint) or service activities (like caring for their area's poor). In addition, the local priest was close to the laity of his village because he often came from a local family and spoke their dialect, which included preaching in the vernacular during Mass. So, in the experience of the overwhelming majority of Christians in these centuries, the face of the Church for laypeople was not a remote and rich cleric, but one of their own who lived and worked with them, sharing their poverty and lay sensibilities.

We should also make the distinction between the relatively few lay aristocrats at the upper crust of society and the very many peasants below. When you read about the laity in the fifth century through the Middle Ages, frequently the monks, theologians, and bishops who are writing are not referring to what we would call blue-collar Christians, but to the highest echelons of society: nobles and royalty. When bishops complain that the laity should have no role in Church affairs, what they mean is not that a parishioner should not complain about a sermon, but that a duke should not try to appoint his brother-in-law as an abbot or bishop, and thereby try to control the Church's power, money, and influence.

Of course, some of these richer laity were well-disposed to the Church and gave huge amounts of money and effort to build churches, convents, monasteries, and centers of learning to spread the Faith. Starting in the fourth century, Roman emperors in the eastern half of the Empire called for regional and ecumenical Church councils and paid the expenses of the traveling bishops, theologians, and advisers who were both clergy and lay. The Byzantine empress Irene called, supervised, and even addressed an extremely consequential general council, Nicaea II in 787, which solved the iconoclast controversy by ruling that Christians could venerate relics and icons. Charlemagne, who ruled most of central Europe in the late 700s and early 800s, was a great protector of the Faith as a layman. His centers of learning, which trained priests and lay scholars, promoted both partnership and tension between clergy and laity. He and his son, Louis the Pious, were seen as new Constantines who endowed the churches, protected the poor, promoted higher learning as well as basic catechesis, and tried to mediate disputes so peace, justice, and the Faith might spread.

Activism and criticism

The Church in the Middle Ages witnessed a solidification of clerical and lay roles. When we visit museums, libraries, or cathedrals, the art and architecture may make us think that only literate monks and bishops dominated medieval Christianity, but side-by-side with the golden age of Christianity in the Middle Ages was a vibrant laity of men and women involved in apostolic acts, confraternities, pilgrimages, religious festivals, and a wide range of other activities.

First, let's talk about the delineations between laity and clergy. As with the later centuries of the first millennium, there was a legitimate concern on the part of Church leaders to restrict lay interference in the appointment of bishops and abbots, and the goal was a positive one—to keep the Church free from outside interference. The laity concerned in this issue were the very few nobles at the highest, wealthiest, and most powerful level of society. In 1296, for instance, Pope Boniface VIII in a papal bull named *Clericis laicos* said harshly:

"That laymen have been very hostile to the clergy antiquity relates; and it is clearly proved by the experiences of the present time. For not content with what is their own the laity strive for what is forbidden and loose the reins for things unlawful." What he was protesting was an attempt by France's king to tax the clergy without papal approval. Clearly, the laity in *Clericis laicos* refers not to the many Christians in the pews, but to the very few on thrones.

The Church's general councils, especially the four Lateran Councils held in the century from 1123 to 1215, issued many canons and disciplinary decrees concerning the clergy that seem intended to separate them from the laity. These canons noted the qualifications for ordination. They also restricted clergy from dressing as laypeople and from taking part in worldly activities such as gambling, acting, and being involved in activities that included the shedding of blood like fighting in the army. In seeking to regulate their conduct and dress, these rules ended up making a very clear demarcation between clergy and laity. This division unfortunately perpetuated the idea that the clerical state was higher than living and working as a layman or woman. But it may have been that the Church's bishops were merely trying to be clear: this is what the clergy and the laity are and are not, what they should and should not do. Fair enough.

Second, and more positively, there were many lay religious activities that separated their activities from clerical ministries. The medieval layman and woman certainly did not live a sterile, Sunday-only faith. Christianity was a vibrant and daily exercise, since the Middle Ages lived and breathed the Faith. The many saints' days, especially local ones, were holidays; in towns, church bells marked time. They couldn't have used these terms, but they lived the spirit of Vatican II's 1965 document *Gaudium et spes* by linking their daily work lives in the world with their faith. They prayed for good crops, gave offerings to local shrines, and celebrated the bigger feast days by staging, acting in, or attending morality plays, passion plays, and lives of the saints. Many of these activities were held at the same time as harvest festivals, liturgical seasons like Advent and Lent, and the major feasts of Christmas and Easter.

We also find in this period an increase in the number of laypeople who were being recognized as saints, first in their communities, then by the bishop nearby, and finally through Rome's procedures for canonization. One study has shown that a fair number of medieval laypeople were declared saints, making them models and heroes for everyone in the Church. Lay brothers and sisters in monasteries in convents along with royalty and nobles won canonization, which might be expected, but so too were lay soldiers, merchants, bankers, shopkeepers, artisans, male and female peasants, and housewives. In the Middle Ages, the number of clerical saints dropped while the relative percentage of lay saints rose. There were more women saints and a greater number from humble origins. Nearly half of all royal saints were female, and women saints were often recognized for their roles as healers and miracle workers.

One of the largest movements in the Middle Ages was a lay upsurge in spirituality called the poor men's movements in which men, and sometimes women, decided to live a radical life of poverty and preaching. They reacted against the worldliness of the upper clergy—meaning the bishops in the larger cities, the cardinals, and the pope—by reaching into the Gospels to find a Christianity that is pure when it is poor. Although some of the movement's followers crossed into heresy and preached even though they did not have a Church license to do so, the majority were orthodox believers who wanted to identify with Christ as much as possible in their daily, lay lives.

Laymen and women were also attracted to the kind of everyday spirituality represented by the *devotio moderna* of the late fourteenth century in northern Europe, where the textile industry was flourishing. They followed the exhortations of preachers who encouraged working-class people to look upon their lay state as workers, husbands and wives, and mothers and fathers as their unique, holy vocations and not as a state of Christian life lower than the clergy's. Unfortunately, this attitude sometimes translated into too much criticism of the clergy. Some priests, bishops, and cardinals were worldly and wealthy, to be sure, but they were not the majority. However, some of the more radical laypeople began to taint all of the clergy, including the poor priests in their own villages and towns, with the unseemly actions of a minority of higher clergy. This criticism, which was certainly justified in some situations but not in all, in the worst case translated into anti-clericalism among some laity. Now, it was the laity and not the Church leaders who were increasing the divide between laity and clergy, a situation that would have difficult ramifications in the Reformation centuries ahead.

If you read Martin Luther's *Ninety-Five Theses* (1517) and the many other reform sermons and scholastic treatises detailing what was wrong with the Church in the fifteenth and sixteenth centuries, you would find yourself agreeing with a fair portion of it—at least in theory, if not in degree. There was an old line that history professors used to use: the Protestant Reformation was caused by bad priests. While it is true that there were immoral and worldly clergy members, especially in the highest power positions, this sentiment is an exaggeration. In fact, recent scholarship illustrates that laypeople and the priests who lived among them were calling for reform because of rising and not falling expectations and standards.

Literacy was on the rise at this time. With the new printing press making little pamphlets affordable, a kind of popular press—the tabloids of their day—hit the scene exactly when Protestants and Catholics were arguing about what kind of Church they saw as authentic. For those who couldn't read, inexpensive woodcuts in the pamphlets got the message across just as well. In addition, Martin Luther (1483–1546) published his criticisms, changes, and ideas on the Church in German, and Jean Calvin (1509–1564) did the same in French, so people could read in their own languages and didn't need to know Latin to be involved in the conversations and debates. Bibles were translated, too, so Christians could read them, especially the Gospels and Paul's key writings, for themselves—although the trouble was that very few understood how to interpret Scripture, which didn't stop them from trying. In this same vein, Protestants said almost anyone could preach, and laypeople with very little learning began to spread a range of ideas.

These were very active, not passive laypeople who saw their faiths as something to be lived and not just followed. A large majority of laypeople, starting in the Middle Ages, were criticizing clergy not because they wanted to get rid of priesthood or bishops, but because they felt some members were not living the way they should. This sentiment was behind criticisms of the Dutch humanist Erasmus (1466–1536), which predated Luther's by a few years. He was often harsh on bad priests, but very encouraging toward laypeople, whom he said should be fully Christian wherever God had placed them. Erasmus wanted weavers and plowmen to sing the psalms in their workshops and fields. Not only men, but women, too, should read the Gospels and Paul's letters. Ditch diggers, Erasmus said, should know theology and the truths of the Faith, which is their birthright as baptized Christians.

When positive (and sometimes justified) criticism of priests crossed into anti-clericalism, troubles began. Some laypeople thought that all Christians were priests and that there should not be any division whatsoever between laity and clergy. Luther taught that ministry was an office or a function, but that it was not necessary to have a class of people, the clergy, set aside to exercise this office or function. Priesthood, for Luther, was not a state or a sacrament and priests should be appointed (not ordained) by the people (not the hierarchy), and not necessarily for their whole lives. Luther taught that baptism makes everyone a priest because all Christians share in the duties and powers of the priesthood of Christ, who is the one and only true priest that the Church needs. The only indelible mark is that of the baptized Christian; ordination did not change a person forever. Anyone could celebrate sacraments and preach, provided they had been properly selected and commissioned, although Luther restricted this function to men and excluded women from ministry.

These ideas are behind the phrase "the priesthood of all believers." Depending on your perspective, this concept either elevated the laity to the status of clergy or reduced the clergy to the status of laypeople—and both perspectives, of course, propagated the idea of a hierarchy of vocations. In fact, however, both Protestants and Catholics turned to lay and priestly formation, although from very different perspectives, in the years after the first generation of the Protestant Reformations in the first half of the sixteenth century. The idea of laity and lay vocation spread quickly and positively throughout the Protestant churches. Many leading laymen were, in fact, former priests, and not all of them continued in ministry: they became theologians, lawyers, and merchants, especially in the book trade as artists, writers, translators, and printers. Their influence and impact were enormous.

Meanwhile, the Catholic Church at the Council of Trent reaffirmed priesthood as a sacrament with an indelible mark and reasserted that priests could not marry and had to be celibate. In addition, Trent said the clergy was indeed a separate category apart from the laity, and absolutely asserted that only an ordained priest could celebrate the sacraments. Only ordained deacons and priests could preach, as well. But right after Trent adjourned in 1563 and then throughout the next few centuries, bishops also spent a great amount of time, energy, effort, and money in improving catechesis among laypeople. Church leaders trained teachers, many of whom were laymen and women, and organized them into the Confraternity of Christian Doctrine (CCD) of that era. Bishops also focused lay religious activities around confraternities and sodalities, which were groups of like-minded people who were drawn to a particular devotion (Sacred Heart of Jesus, the rosary) or saint (local, like Saint Ambrose in Milan, or universal, like Saint Joseph or Mary). Unlike in the Middle Ages, however, during the Reformation era these lay groups lost some of their independence and autonomy when the Church required them to be affiliated with a certain priest, parish, religious order, or some other ecclesiastical authority. This desire for institutional oversight makes sense given the breakaway of Protestants and the many different ideas contrary to Catholic orthodoxy that were competing with Catholicism and confusing Catholics.

Finally, let's remember that many laypeople, both Protestants and Catholics, died for the Faith in the conflicts and wars fought in the name of religion in these centuries. They were martyrs for Christianity, regardless of their Protestant or Catholic faith. The horrid fact is that Christians were killing Christians.

Being faithful in a changing world

While laypeople for over one thousand five hundred years had struggled to live their Christianity in the face of the idea that a clerical life was somehow higher or better, the early modern period offered new challenges: that of living a religious life at all in a scientific and nationalistic age. In these centuries, European Catholics were on occasion seen as superstitious compared to the rationalism and secularism of the Scientific Revolution and Enlightenment. They were also accused of being ultimately faithful not to their countries, but to the pope. This allegiance competed with the national pride toward one's country that became stronger during this early modern period. Moreover, the French Revolution and similar, smaller outbreaks of violence throughout Europe saw the papacy as another monarchy to be toppled, the clergy as another privileged aristocratic class to be overthrown, and lay Catholics as disloyal aliens to these political and social goals. Clergy and laity were subject to suspicion and assault from enemies outside the Church, while within the Church, one group (laity) shored up their own feelings against the other group (clergy), and vice versa. Meanwhile, in the colonies and empires that followed the age of European exploration, new laypeople entered the Church, which in turn raised novel questions: could slaves and indigenous people receive the Eucharist and fully share in the sacramental life of the Church, for instance, and could the men among them be ordained priests or not?

A renewed spirituality helped laypeople navigate these waters. Francis de Sales (1567–1622) and Jane de Chantal (1572–1641) died on the threshold of early modernity, but their ideas had a lasting impact throughout the period that followed their ministries. In a long friendship whose ideas are preserved in many letters, de Sales and de Chantal called everyone to live the Christian life fully, regardless of their lay or clerical state. In fact, laypeople grabbed onto these ideas a bit more enthusiastically and in greater numbers than the clergy, perhaps because the laity was looking for an identity in these difficult times after the Protestant Reformations and the Council of Trent, which were followed by the Scientific Revolution and new national movements that also challenged faith.

De Sales and de Chantal called laywomen and men to love God as much as they could within one's circumstances—that is, to live a devout life. De Sales described this love as having two arms: one in prayer and one in service. Together, they offered a positive notion of the material world, turning back any remaining notion of *contemptus mundi* from the first millennium and Middle Ages, while anticipating the openness of Vatican II in the 1960s. They gave very practical advice on daily work, marriage, family life and realized that, given the pressures of these obligations, prayer must often be short. That fact, they said, was fine: prayer was good and pleasing to God, especially when charitable service to family and friends was what kept you away from hours of private contemplation. Here are de Sales' two arms at work and in dialogue. For them, the interactions between human beings in the everyday details and ordinary nature of daily life were opportunities for laymen and women to be Christ for each other in humble service and interdependence. One didn't have to perform monastic acts of self-mortification to achieve this goal of purification: doing what nobody else wanted to do—like washing the dishes or scrubbing the laundry or milking the cow at dawn—was a path to God.

From the middle of the nineteenth century, and especially since Vatican II (1962–1965), laypeople have been involved in Church leadership on the largest scale than any other time in Church history. The old line that the laity's job was only to "pray, pay, and obey"—which was probably never as dominant as the cliché goes—has certainly not been true in the modern Church.

The man who gave the laity a kind of justifying theology of his own was, ironically, a member of the clergy: the British priest and later Cardinal John Henry Newman (1801–1890). As a Church historian, he saw in the fourth century a model for lay orthodoxy when he identified the fact that many laypeople kept the true faith in Jesus' humanity and divinity even as some bishops after the Council of Nicaea maintained the condemned Arian heresy that Jesus was not quite God. Newman called for the laity to be well-educated, to be leaders in their parishes and the wider Church, and to be consulted on matters of doctrine. Because he stressed that the entire mystical body of Christ—the Church—holds the Faith firmly and truly, Newman said that when Church authorities were defining doctrine, they should listen to the laypeople to hear what people already believed and have always believed. A British bishop responded to Newman's championing such an essential role for the laity by dismissively asking who the laity even were. Newman famously responded that the Church would look foolish without laymen and women.

Change was certainly in the air during this period. The current Code of Canon Law was revised in 1983 and contains more and greater treatment of the laity than the previous 1917 edition. More attention, and we might even say respect, is paid to laypeople's equality as believers as well as to their rights, particular mission and vocation, and their access to theological formation on basic and advanced levels. Indeed, canon 229, paragraphs 1 and 2 are worth quoting:

"Laypersons are bound by the obligation and possess the right to acquire knowledge of Christian doctrine appropriate to the capacity and condition of each in order for them to be able to live according to this doctrine, announce it themselves, defend it if necessary, and take their part in exercising the apostolate.

"They also possess the right to acquire that fuller knowledge of the sacred sciences which are taught in ecclesiastical universities and faculties or in institutes of religious sciences, by attending classes there and pursuing academic degrees."

While another canon (212, paragraph 1) notes that the laity are obligated to demonstrate obedience to their pastors, paragraph 2 of that same canon says laypeople are free to tell their pastors of their needs and desires, while paragraph 3 says laypeople "have the right and even at times the duty" to give their opinions, based on their experience and knowledge, about matters affecting the Church.

Vatican II devoted a document to the laity, titled *Apostolicam actousitatem*, although the laity appear in many of the fifteen other documents that the council promulgated. *Lumen gentium*, for instance, gave perhaps the clearest and most refreshing sentence on the matter: "The lay apostolate, however, is a participation in the salvific mission of the Church itself. Through their baptism and confirmation all are commissioned to that apostolate by the Lord Himself" (no. 33). This same document sought a greater mutual respect between clergy and laity, asking pastors to allow laypeople to exercise their proper ministries in the parish, while stressing that the laity bore a special duty to share Christianity where they worked, particularly in secular settings.

It was refreshing at the council to hear that laypeople had vocations. Simply using that word "vocation," which too often had been applied exclusively to a priest or nun, raised the prestige and standing of the layperson. Laity learned that they had a special and equal vocation; they weren't simply defined negatively as "not a member of the clergy." Some of the bishops gathered in Rome for the council identified clericalism as an enemy of the Church, which is a reminder that both clericalism and anti-clericalism harm the clergy and laity of the Church in any age.

Apostolicam actuositatem recognized that, in the modern age, the layperson's role had expanded and was growing daily more critical, not only to the Church, but also to the world. The role of laywomen was seen as something that had to grow, become more vital, and move closer to the center of discussions, influence, leadership, and decision-making authority. Another Vatican II document, *Gravissimum educationis*, joined *Apostolicam actuositatem* in stressing that the laity should be well-educated in the Faith and that they played a key educational role as teachers, catechists, and parents. Significantly, the document on the liturgy, *Sacrosanctum concilium*, called for the laity's active participation in liturgy; the ecumenical document, *Unitatis redintegratio*, identified the lay tasks in reaching out to people of other faiths; and the document on bishops, *Christus dominus*, encouraged them to promote and support the lay vocation and apostolate.

Not only have lay Catholics transformed the Faith, but they have moved into leadership roles in their countries, too. In the United States, for instance, Catholics moved away from the attacks upon them as immigrants. Once known and feared as the "Catholic hordes"—immigrants from the middle of the nineteenth to the beginning of the twentieth centuries—laypeople have left the "Catholic ghetto" to which they had been consigned and are now major players in business, education, economics, and politics. Catholics sit on the United States Supreme Court, have occupied the Oval Office, fill boardrooms and judicial benches, teach at every educational level, and are clearly in the mainstream of American culture and power. What lay Catholics do with that power in both Church and civil arenas will be part of the next, unwritten chapter of Church history.

Discussion questions

- What surprised you about how lay activity has changed over the centuries?

- What examples of lay spirituality and participation in Church affairs do you think the Church should leave behind? Why?

- What examples of lay spirituality and participation in Church affairs do you think the Church should recover? Why?

- What is the state of lay leadership and participation today? If you think it should change, how might that happen?

- Where do you think lay activity should go in the future?

Epilogue

MAKING HISTORY

WHILE MOST PEOPLE like to think the Church has always been the same, even a quick glance through Church history demonstrates the exact opposite: the only constant in Church history is change itself. By looking at how the Church developed her structures, beliefs, Scriptures, Mass and sacraments, relations with other faiths, and the role of the laity, hopefully we've discovered a bit about how the Church has tried to balance her old treasures with new discoveries for two thousand years as she's made history.

The Church has at times turned her back to the world when challenged, to be sure, but at other moments she has been at her most innovative when faced with new situations. Almost from the start of Christianity, for example, questions about doctrine pressed theologians and bishops to come up with clearer and better descriptions of the Faith, which in turn led to more questions and deeper thinking. As time passed, whenever Christians met non-Christians— particularly in Asia, Africa, and the Americas as the first millennium turned into the second and traveled through the age of European exploration—she asked herself how these indigenous peoples were to be treated, were they adults or children, and who would be responsible for the Faith in their region. So each chapter of Church history follows the past in a cycle of new experiences that build on previous beliefs and practices.

This process of reframing old treasures in new language continues to thrive. For instance, the modern Church practices many and varied spiritualities. Devotions such as eucharistic adoration and the rosary are enjoying a renewed popularity that dipped a bit after Vatican II but are finding a new audience in a younger generation of Catholics that was not raised with these practices. Meanwhile, the Catholic trend right after Vatican II to experiment with eastern religions such as Buddhism continues, and there are especially interesting links being made in the realms of mysticism, meditation, and prayer that enrich each tradition and promote interreligious dialogue, understanding, and respect. What this means is that the last one hundred fifty years or so of Church history have witnessed continued testing and adaptation at the same time that spirituality grounded in the past remains popular, too. There's room for both within the practice of Roman Catholicism.

Still, it cannot be denied that the Church is still faced by the Enlightenment challenges of secularism and materialism. Faith competes with rationalism and atheism; some Christians (and people of all faiths, for that matter) find it hard to be taken seriously in their careers when they reveal themselves to be people of belief. In Europe, especially, it appears that the Christian heritage has fallen away from people's minds: some fail to see that for the entire history of Europe since the Roman Empire, Christianity was the glue of society. Elsewhere, other gods like drugs and alcohol have seized people's lives. There is a litany of statistics to show Church attendance is down, but while this may be true in Europe and North America, it is not true in Asia, Africa, and Latin and South America, where local forms of spirituality, liturgy, and devotions take the Church in lively directions.

At the same time, the Church has taken steps to demonstrate that she is not hiding behind a wall of blind, deaf, and dumb faith. Pope John Paul II, a former university professor, wrote an encyclical titled *Faith and Reason*, which put this long-standing tension in context: faith and reason need not be in competition today nor have they been in Church history. He also said that evolution is not incompatible with the idea that God created the world. He, of all people, certainly did not fail to embrace new media technology to skillfully spread the Gospel. And, most spectacularly, the Church has not distanced itself from facing down economic systems that challenge faith and human rights. The same pope who helped defeat Communism was one of capitalism's biggest critics, too.

We should add that all religious faith, including Christianity, is not, contrary to conventional wisdom, doing poorly. The coming of the third millennium and current debates about faith and public life demonstrate that religion as a cultural factor is still strong. While these events may have illustrated some of the negatives connected with religion—one thinks of millennial cults and the somewhat paganistic elements of the New Age—at the same time they show religion's enduring attraction. Only hungry people hunt for spirituality. That hunt shows that traditional religions may not be satisfying the human hunger for God, but the hunt simultaneously demonstrates the fact that spirituality has not been abandoned wholesale, either. It is a good, not a bad time for religion, but it means that Christianity has to find up-to-date ways to spread an ancient faith.

Similarly, as in past eras, during modernity the Church has had to think about its relationship with a changing world. For example, the early medieval *contemptus mundi* gave way to an evangelical embrace of the world with Francis of Assisi. Continuing this trend, Catholics have embraced the idea of social Catholicism since the nineteenth century. As in the Middle Ages, modern laypeople especially tried to take care of society's castoffs, to look after the poor and refugees of war, and to make sure that Christ is alive in the ghettos and among new immigrants. Vatican II asked Catholics to embrace the world more fully in its groundbreaking document *Gaudium et spes*, saying that the Church lived with the world's joys, hopes, and sorrows, but this was nothing new in terms of direction. The institutional Church was only saying more boldly and explicitly than ever before what laypeople and parish priests had been living at the grass-roots level for centuries.

Indeed, it's sometimes been the people in the Church's pews who have been ahead of the curve in making history. The trustee movement in American Church history remains controversial, but the idea of lay boards being more deeply involved in a deliberative way and not just receiving *fait accompli* decisions from pastors and bishops resonates in the aftermath of the sexual abuse revelations of the last decades. Looking back with admittedly twenty-twenty hindsight, we can fairly ask whether priest-pedophiles would have been so easily moved by their bishops to new parishes where they continued to abuse children had laypeople, specifically working-class parents with children in parochial schools, sat on priest personnel boards. The story of lay trusteeism is a difficult chapter in Church history, but that doesn't mean positive lessons of the kind of real collaboration, collegiality, and unprecedented lay participation that are clearly needed today can't be drawn from nineteenth-century American Church history.

Finally, the Church is at a critical moment in her internal life when it comes to Vatican II. Unfortunately, the Church is seen too often like a political body, with so-called conservatives and liberals fighting for control on the edges, with an increasingly smaller middle ground overlooked. In truth, modern political labels like these just don't work when applied to the Church. Catholic bishops are typically conservative when it comes to doctrine—it's their job, after all, to preserve the Faith—but on matters like social justice, workers' rights, and war and peace, the Church falls along the progressive end of the spectrum. True, in the decade after Vatican II, progressive changes happened quickly and frequently without good explanations backing them up. That was followed in the 1980s and 1990s by a natural pendulum swing in the other direction, with some calling for a wholesale return to the Latin Mass and a mythic good-old-days in the belief that turning back the clock will magically sweep away the Church's contemporary challenges. Some Catholics say that Vatican II was a mistake, while others claim the council's agenda has been cast aside and stymied. This scenario is a false dichotomy of extreme positions that does no one any good.

There are two ways to look at this situation: as a quagmire or as an opportunity. We could lament that the Church is irrevocably divided against herself and leave the battles to the wings. Alternately, we could decide that both ends of the spectrum have a hold on part of the picture, have something to teach the other end, but also have something to learn from the other end. That takes humility, a lost virtue that needs to be recovered and is a great gift of studying Church history. This second, humble way of looking at this situation—as an opportunity—should be the way to go, since history teaches that the Council of Trent faced a similar challenge in the sixteenth century. It was by finding the balance that the Church was able to move forward after Trent. She remembered what she taught, explained her doctrines more clearly, embraced the opportunities to evangelize in the New Worlds being discovered, cleaned up some of the mess of arithmetical piety, established better schools for priests and educational systems for laypeople, and committed herself to doing a better job by admitting (if only quietly and to herself) that mistakes had been made. It may be, then, that the Church's greatest challenge is not behind her, but ahead. The history yet to be made just might see the Church's believers doing now what they've often done in the past: find the acceptable middle way, strike the balance, and continue walking in the light of faith.

Sources Cited

All statements from the *Code of Canon Law*, Vatican II, Pius XII, Paul VI, and John Paul II are taken from www.vatican.va.

Chapter 1

Ignatius of Antioch: Boniface Ramsey, *Beginning to Read the Fathers* (New York: Paulist Press, 1985), pp. 109–110.

Cyprian: Henry Bettenson, ed., *Documents of the Christian Church*, 2d ed. (London: Oxford University Press, 1967), p. 72.

Julius I: Henry Bettenson, ed., *Documents of the Christian Church*, 2d ed. (London: Oxford University Press, 1967), p. 79.

Council of Constance: Henry Bettenson, ed., *Documents of the Christian Church*, 2d ed. (London: Oxford University Press, 1967), p. 135.

Pius II: Henry Bettenson, ed., *Documents of the Christian Church*, 2d ed. (London: Oxford University Press, 1967), p. 136.

Chapter 6

Gregory the Great: J. Barmby, trans., *A Select Library of Nicene and Post-Nicene Fathers. Second Series, XIII* (New York: The Christian Literature Co., 1898), pp. 84–85.

Bernard of Clairvaux: James Bruno Scott, trans., *The Letters of St. Bernard of Clairvaux* (London: Burns & Oates, 1953), p. 462.

Propagation of the Faith in Asia: Wolfgang Müller, et al, eds. *The Church in the Age of Absolutism and Enlightenment,* trans. Gunther J. Holst (New York: Crossroad, 1981), p. 286.

Chapter 7

Boniface VIII: Henry Bettenson, ed., *Documents of the Christian Church*, 2d ed. (London: Oxford University Press, 1967), p. 113.

Other Related Liguori Publications Titles...

Also by Christopher M. Bellitto, PhD

Church History 101
A Concise Overview
ISBN: 978-0-7648-1603-1

This easy-to-read volume answers the basic question, "what did the Church look like in this particular period?" for the four traditionally recognized eras of Church history: early, medieval, Reformation, and modern. Each chapter includes a map and timeline to locate the reader in time and place. The timeline identifies what else was going on. Then they address these topics: 1) The Big Picture: a broad overview of the era; 2) The Church's Hierarchy: a look at the popes, cardinals, and bishops with their concerns; 3) The Church in the Pews: what was Christianity like for the average person; and 4) What made this period unique—taking a comparative approach. All chapters conclude with discussion questions and a list for further reading.

Liturgy 101
Sacraments and Sacramentals
Daniel G. Van Slyke STL, PhD

ISBN: 978-0-7648-1845-5

Respected Catholic scholar and educator Daniel G. Van Slyke grounds *Liturgy 101* in sacred Scripture, the teachings of the Church, and the rites with which the Church celebrates the sacraments. Each chapter explains the sacrament's origins, how and by whom it is celebrated, and what it accomplishes. Van Slyke also addresses frequently asked pastoral, practical, and canonical questions concerning the celebration of the sacraments.

To order visit your local bookstore or call 800-325-9521
or visit us at www.liguori.org